A God for this World

A God for this World

Scott Cowdell

MOWBRAY

London and New York

Mowbray
A Continuum imprint
Wellington House, 125 Strand, London WC2R 0BB
370 Lexington Avenue, New York, NY 10017–6503

First published 2000

British Library Cataloguing-in-Publication Data
A catalogue record for this book is available from the British Library.

ISBN 0–264–67509–6 (hardback)
   0–264–67501–0 (paperback)

Library of Congress Cataloging-in-Publication Data
Cowdell, Scott.
  A God for this world/Scott Cowdell.
    p. cm.
  Includes bibliographical references and index.
  ISBN 0–264–67509–6 (hb) — ISBN 0–264–67501–0 (pbk.)
  1. God. 2. Christian Life—Anglican authors. I. Title
  BT102.C69 2000
  231.7—dc21   99–055355

Typeset by York House Typographic Ltd
Printed and bound in Great Britain by Biddles Ltd, Guildford and King's Lynn

To the faculty, staff,
students and recent graduates of
St Barnabas' Theological College, Adelaide

Let the word of Christ dwell in you richly;
teach and admonish one another in all wisdom;
and with gratitude in your hearts sing psalms,
hymns and spiritual songs to God.

Colossians 3.16

Well, I said, better to wait
for him on some peninsula
of the spirit. Surely for one
with patience he will happen by
once in a while. It was the heart
spoke. The mind, sceptical as always
of the anthropomorphisms
of the fancy, knew he must be put together
like a poem or a composition
in music, that what he conforms to
is art. A promontory is a bare
place; no God leans down
out of the air to take the hand
extended to him. The generations have
watched there
in vain. We are beginning to see
now it is matter is the scaffolding
of spirit; that the poem emerges
from morphemes and phonemes; that
as form in sculpture is the prisoner
of the hard rock, so in everyday life
it is the plain facts and natural happenings
that conceal God and reveal him to us
little by little under the mind's tooling.

R. S. Thomas, 1913–, 'Emerging'

Contents

Preface

This is a book about how to imagine God in relationship with the world as we now know it, a world understood increasingly on its own terms: holistic, secular, terrible, yes, but also wonderful – *our* world. It is a book about rediscovering a sense of lively connection between God and the world which used to be a feature of Christian faith, but which has increasingly given way to a remote God and the rise of an understandable atheism since the seventeenth century. It is a book that looks for God beyond such remote imagery and its atheistic shadow, in conversation with the latest science but also with the long tradition of faith. It is a book about a God who continually creates, loves and honours the world, at work 'in, with and under' the struggles of matter, life and consciousness.

This book is written at a time of uncertainty about theology's role in the life of the Church, or at least within Australian Anglicanism. Faced by dwindling congregations and an indifferent society, the Church naturally yearns to recover an edge, to enliven its practice and revitalize its structures. 'Relevance' is everywhere the catchcry – 'they seek it here, they seek it there' – but not, I fear, at sufficient depth. For surely theology remains the key for faith and proclamation, not an adjunct, not a luxury, nor less a distraction from the main game. Hence these labours: to identify some of the problems that have undermined faith in God, to point toward emerging alternatives, to think about the relationship of God and the world in a new context, marked by new currents in science, in culture, in sensibility – all of which will hopefully encourage faith and imagination today.

Feast of Saints Peter & Paul   Scott Cowdell
Apostles & Martyrs   Adelaide
29 June 1999

Acknowledgements

I owe a debt of gratitude to Professor Ian Markham, of Liverpool Hope University College, who urged me to pursue this project, my having tried out the initial idea on him in mid-1997 when I was teaching theology at Trinity College within the University of Melbourne and he was a Visiting Fellow. Ian's critical efforts with the original proposal and the final manuscript, at the behest of my publisher, are much appreciated. Speaking of whom, I thank Ruth McCurry at Continuum in London for her enthusiasm over the project and for seeing it on its way. Four others kindly took time over the first draft. My St Barnabas' colleague Dr Duncan Reid, my friend (and one-time training rector) Canon Lyall Turley and Australia's senior Anglican theologian, Archbishop Peter Carnley, all made helpful comments. My old friend Dr Peter Farrell, now of the Optical Technology Research Laboratory at Victoria University in Melbourne, kindly cast a physicist's eye over Chapter 5, and gave it his imprimatur. Peter is a good atheist, and I was delighted at this opportunity to continue a conversation we began twenty years ago, when we were physics undergraduates together. All these kind people have done both writer and reader an important service.

For her patience and support I thank my secretary, Mrs Barbara Dalton, and also Ms Beth Prior, who serves our unique ecumenical campus here at the Adelaide College of Divinity as Librarian, and has been most helpful to me, even when I've been a nuisance. Last of all I thank my wife Lisa Carley, who has once again read through a manuscript for me, for her gift to me of a constant heart.

Poetry from *R. S. Thomas: Collected Poems 1945–1990* (1993) (London: Phoenix Giant, 1995) is used with kind permission of the publisher. This ancient priest and poet discerns a living God within deep folds of the ordinary, despite an often bleak vision in which doubt and faith are woven fine. Might R. S. Thomas be Anglicanism's most profound witness in this present time?

My cover illustration, 'The Dome', is by Jeffrey Smart, the elder statesman of Australian painting, now based in Tuscany. It is reproduced with his kind permission. His haunting canvasses, often of existentially bleak modern scenes, pulsate with an eerie sense that something transcendent is present. With typical Australian scepticism Smart prefers to evaluate his work in technical, compositional terms. But despite this disclaimer, I am far from alone in interpreting it as that of a profoundly spiritual artist.

I dedicate this book to the theological college which I lead, and to its people, at a time when the challenge of integrating theology with spirituality and ministry is most pressing, for the sake of both the Church and the world.

Part I

At Home in the World?

1 The Context of Belief

Is there a place
here for the spirit? Is there time
on this brief platform for anything
other than the mind's failure to explain itself?

R. S. Thomas, 'Balance'

It so happens that I begin writing this first chapter on the Feast of Epiphany. At the Eucharist early this morning the wise men were once again at the crib, with the star hanging in tribute to the enlightening of their minds and hearts. The long search of the wise seeker has an ending, according to the Christian vision, a fulfilment. Epiphany unashamedly points the questing intellect and the restless imagination to God,[1] and moreover to a God disclosed in the peculiarity, indeed in the scandal, of historical particularity and what we might call speculative insufficiency. Yet Epiphany is not embarrassed by the enormity of its claims; the conviction behind the Gospel account, borne out subsequently by many of history's greatest intellects, is that all wisdom and insight is somehow gathered, corrected and completed in the Church's Gospel of a Triune God.

But on returning home from the Eucharist and opening my morning paper over breakfast, I was reminded of how ludicrous all this sounds to many intelligent people. In one article the leading science presenter on national radio was interviewed about his religious scepticism, and how he 'passed on disbelief' to his children. His argument seemed to consist of a native dislike of authoritarianism (religious or otherwise), a strong vein of protest atheism unable to reconcile 'any sort of beneficent Christian God plus Auschwitz', and an empiricist's rejection of claims for an intervening supernatural being: 'There is no evidence for it. And so I find it in some ways intellectually insulting', he says.[2]

As is normally the case when confronted by these common enough concerns, my heart sank. Does he not know that countless Christian believers oppose religious and political authoritarianism, and this from the heart of their faith and their churches, rather than the disaffected fringes? Does he not know that theology has long struggled to answer protest atheism, at least since Job rejected an overoptimistic Deuteronomic history, and Israel's prophets dreamed of hope in exile, and the discontinuity of crucifixion marked Christianity's emergent understanding of divine power? Indeed, does he not know that belief is often strongest in suffering? Has he not happened upon an impromptu shrine the faithful have set up at Auschwitz in the death cell of Father Maximilian Kolbe? And does he not know that the closed world of immutable scientific law, that perennial breeding ground of hardbitten sceptics, is more a feature of late seventeenth- than of late twentieth-century science, in the same way that God as a remote super-natural person is more a feature of seventeenth- than of twentieth-century theology?

I am not angry at this sceptical 'man of science' – indeed, I usually prefer a good atheist to a lukewarm believer, because I often discern an intention toward robust faith behind the rejection of naive divinity. But I am dis-appointed that Christians have prized and in many cases tenaciously maintained images of God that positively invite religious scepticism, and with these images a penumbra of untenable and improper secondary beliefs about Church, worship and life in the world. Priests and parents, Sunday School teachers and even theologians have bound heavy burdens of belief, hard to bear, in commending images of God which fail to resonate power-fully with experience, images of God which are remote from life in the world. The star of Epiphany leads the honest seeker on an energizing journey toward understanding and imaginative satisfaction. Many, however, have looked to the Church and its presentation of Christian belief, and have failed to find a guiding star which thrills them and beckons them on.

Many will share my experience of listening to a certain sort of unbeliever and finding myself in considerable agreement, here applauding an unsenti-mental view of life in the world, there agreeing that the God they reject ought to be rejected, while still able to commend 'the Christian God', which is not being rejected because it is not the understanding of God in contention. With the sceptical 'man of science', whose opinions greeted me at breakfast, many Christians share a deep love of freedom, experience disquiet in the face of cosmic indifference and human evil and relate to both scientific and historical truth with intellectual integrity, yet they still believe. Clearly the God they believe in is not remote from life nor incompatible with the often bitter facts of life. It is a God remote from the wellsprings of creativity, joy and responsibility that is often rejected, irreconcilable with the deepest understandings and commitments that life in the world evokes.

A theological agenda

What are some key aspects of life in the world that demand theological account be taken of them, some plain facts in our present context from which Christian faith ought not to resile?

It should be made clear at the outset that the perspective of particular human subjects looms large in any conception of life's key themes and dominant realities. Where once we could erroneously assume that white, male, educated, affluent Western experience was normative, for instance, today's postmodern sensibility brings a diversity of human realities to light. So for example a modern and in particular a romantic tendency toward finding life's meaning 'within', and a personal conception of experience, is challenged by politically charged accounts of human reality from the economic margins of the reflective, leisured world, and from the perspective of a gender inequality which it frequently overlooks. Correspondingly, many careful historical studies have sufficiently deconstructed dominant accounts of experience that one needs to be cautious about generalizations. Every minority group now insists on its own version of things being heard, its own story. This is true of women, of indigenous peoples, of 'Africans of the diaspora', of 'women of colour', of lesbians and gay men. Each of these groups now champions its own accounts of history, of race, of sexuality, of human being, thus asserting its claim against the entrenched narratives and taboos that have marginalized it.

Christian apologetics should be chastened by its encounter with this newly minted sense of human diversity, in particular the strongly emergent discourses of otherness – those stories and perspectives which have been unknown or repressed thanks to the dominance of other stories and perspectives. Apologetics must leave off grimly insisting on a particular version of the human condition to which its particular slant on Christianity offers the definitive answer. Nowadays such a strategy convinces fewer and fewer people, and can contribute to marginalizing parts of the human family by overlooking key perspectives.

With this warning in mind I will venture to identify three points of reference we might still consider to be central, as long as sufficient care is taken not to overgeneralize. They are, first, the awareness of structural evil and human vulnerability; second, the emerging scientific and cultural holism which reconceives reality in terms of fundamental relatedness; and, third, the widening experience of secularity.

Structural evil and human vulnerability appear with a new clarity in the postmodern context. No longer does the Western world believe that inexorable historical forces are on its side. The myth of progress, a chief building block of the modern world, has now collapsed into a mood of anxiety and uncertainty throughout the West, in every realm but that of technology's unreflective onward swagger. We are on our own, against the odds.

The emerging conception of reality as holistic and fundamentally relational is a cultural phenomenon with its roots in the natural sciences, in particular physics and biology, along with the human sciences of sociology, anthropology and linguistics. While it may be said that these are rarefied and privileged discourses that do not shape the subjectivity of most human beings in the world, nevertheless these perceptions are becoming a part of the *Zeitgeist*. Thinking relationally about reality is more and more intellectually and even spiritually compelling, so it is appropriate to include it among the main coordinates of life in today's world.

Secularity is a major factor in the way today's Westerners experience the world, and increasingly people in traditional Roman Catholic societies like Spain, along with Orthodox countries such as Russia now emerging from their Communist past. While a certain post-secular re-enchanting of the world is now taking place, nevertheless the kind of human experiences possible in the religiously charged, prescientific and pagan world are no longer accessible. They defeated even the romantic incredulity of late twentieth-century syncretism to recapture them.

Taking these three themes in order we now consider them in greater detail. In particular we will be alert as to how inadequate images of God contribute to unbelief in each of these areas, as they stifle profound engagement with the realities in question.

Evil and suffering

First we note the brute realities of human vulnerability, wickedness and intransigence, of natural disaster and the mute agonies of countless billions among our non-human fellow travellers, all of which have so profoundly challenged Christian images of an all-powerful, all-caring God. And with this goes the now widespread sense that humanity can and should secure its own future, rather than trust passively in divine providence. Hence the so-called problem of evil.

The problem of evil plays a major role in the philosophy of religion, and theodicy – the attempt to justify God's goodness against the problem of evil – has been an established part of Christian apologetics since the eighteenth century. Western literature of the twentieth century was familiar with the struggle to maintain life's meaning and dignity in the face of its apparent denial in a vast and largely inhospitable universe. The existentialists are particularly aware of this burden, with Dostoyevsky[3] and Camus[4] offering classic versions of the dilemma. The enormity and unprofitability of so much suffering cries out to heaven, and where is the providential deity? Better to abandon that wish-fulfilling dream and maintain human value as best we can, without the supernatural – neither as support for the present nor as hope for the future. This bold decision to 'rage against the dying of the light' is the anguished nobility of existentialism and protest atheism, though one might discern an implicit faith within it that keeps nihilism at bay, the sort of 'fundamental trust' Hans Küng for one places at the heart of his Christian apologetics.[5]

No longer can we delude ourselves that our person, our family, our tribe, our nation or indeed our world has a particular advantage against the forces of nature and human culpability. Who is now confident of special supernatural protection? Even those who claim the intervening support of God are themselves more than likely to be found striving against the natural, political and social enemies of human thriving and ecological sustainability. Where nowadays is the passive believer serenely looking out on a static world, waiting expectantly for divine blessings to flow? At least in the West we now expect to take a hand in securing our own future through the political, economic and social opportunities that democratic institutions and the late capitalist economy allow. And at last we are learning that without our best efforts this fragile planet Earth may be fatally compromised, and we with it. Looking back over the war-ravaged, blood-soaked twentieth century, and looking forward with newly acquired global and ecological spectacles, none of us I suggest are expecting miraculous deliverance. If God is at work in our world it cannot be as an all-powerful deliverer. Maurice Wiles, among many who have raised the question, asks why there are not more miracles, and better ones, if God is like that?[6] So the theologian shares the concern of the atheist, as honesty and human fellow feeling demands. But this theological protest is not a despairing one, as it brings with it new images of God and new understandings of divine action, approaches that if they cannot fully explicate divine action at least make it less incomprehensible – less irreconcilable with the 'heart of darkness' humanity now perceives, and with the dogged solidarity to which humanity must now aspire. In later chapters we will seek images of God and of God's action which are less remote from human experience and from human vocation today.

A holistic vision

We proceed now to our second consideration, noting the significant change in world-view that is emerging from the natural and social sciences. And once again we see the extent to which rejection of God means rejection of God-images that are remote from the world and from human reality.

The world seen as a hierarchy, a 'great chain of being', is no more. Science arose in the early Enlightenment of the seventeenth century offering a new and more democratic view, a world of entities linked by forces. In the age of revolution human hierarchies were correspondingly disposed of, politically and to some extent socially. Thus began a more relational conception of reality, which came to replace the static and vertically ordered cosmos that had not been fundamentally reconceived since the time of Aristotle and Plato. But even the new scientific cosmos retained aspects of the former rigidity, presenting a law-governed mechanistic fixity.

With quantum physics, special relativity and general relativity early in the twentieth century, however, came an end to all such rigid imagery. The world of Newton and Laplace, a world of synchronous clocks, of particles like billiard balls in thoroughly predictable motion, of reality as an ordered ensemble, was completely revised. Modern physics goes beyond earlier science and gives us everything overlapped and related. Time and space are two sides of the one coin, as are matter and energy, while the world can be conceived of in terms of fields as readily as particles. Famously, the positions of electrons and photons of energy have to be determined statistically. So the hard-edged sense of individual objects, which is familiar to us from the scale of our experience, is no longer a helpful image at the subatomic scale.[7] Moreover, the physics of the atom, and of the two fundamental natural forces which are only discernible at atomic distances (the 'strong force' holding together the nucleus and the 'weak force' evident in the behaviour of electrons – the other two fundamental forces being the gravitational and electromagnetic forces), are inextricably linked with the physics of the very large, with astrophysics. The search for the 'Big Bang' is a search for the origin of our universe in inconceivably small spaces over immeasurably short microfractions of a millisecond, yet at incredibly high temperatures, and some fifteen thousand million years ago (thirteen billion is a more recent best guess). And the signature of this primal event, this 'singularity', can be read off the face of the universe still as an ambient background temperature. So physics at the levels of quantum tininess and cosmological vastness meshes together in attempts to understand the emergence, evolution and eventual fate of our universe – everything is related to everything else.[8]

But these new insights of science are not confined to the realms of the impossibly small and the inconceivably vast. The newer and not entirely helpfully named area of physics and mathematics called chaos theory takes a fresh look at phenomena in the everyday world that we experience. It uncovers a far more unsettled and touchy state of affairs than Newton's physics ever imagined. It builds on the recognition that many natural systems display to an extreme extent what physics calls 'sensitivity to initial conditions'. So minuscule changes can blow out to enormous outcomes, in weather patterns, for instance, and in all sorts of dependable regular systems (like turbulent flow in fluids, and the human heartbeat). The flip side of chaos theory has been the discovery of deep order in physical systems that once seemed chaotic, but this too is an expression of reality's fundamental relatedness – of part to part, part to whole and whole to part.[9]

We are not restricted to physics for these insights, which can seem far from the sciences of living things. Modern evolutionary biology and genetics have similar holistic stories to tell. They have defined the human person as firmly embedded within the natural order. Human beings are now known to have emerged from the web of life by evolution through natural selection, where once a special act of divine creation was invoked to account for human distinctiveness. A growing awareness this century that the Earth's biosphere is a linked web of ecosystems heightens our sense that all things cohere, standing and falling together. As a result, a new ecological sensibility and mood of responsibility is growing in the West. Humanity, increasingly owning its place in the natural world, is increasingly owning up to its responsibility for that world.

But there is more to be said here, for the holistic vision is emerging in the human and social sciences as well as in the physical and biological ones. According to emerging postmodern understandings of human life, the collective facts of our life together in communities and cultures play key roles in determining the way human individuals experience and name reality. The independent individual of modernity, albeit a participant in social realities, is overtaken in today's postmodern West by the individual as cultural product, even in certain subcultures as cultural artefact (think of the biker, the punk, the boot-scooting urban cowboy, the bimbo, the gym junkie, the black-clad café set, and any number of faddish off-the-shelf identities and pseudo-communities available in the West today). The world-view imposed by our culture, which we inhabit often unthinkingly from childhood, like the implicate ordering of experience entailed by the particular language we speak, now looms large in accounting for attitudes and perceptions we once assumed were objective and obvious.

Along with all of this comes a radical historicism which is deconstructive of former certainties, and hence deeply sceptical. The seeming obviousness of our defining myths, biases and certainties is laid bare by careful attention to the social, cultural, political and economic conditions from which they arose. Often they are found to rest on unreliable and questionable foundations – not infrequently on ideologies of social control (think for instance of our gender and racial stereotypes). This has the effect of relativizing our convictions, ushering in 'an age of critical theories'. With this dawning recognition that for good and ill our experience is heavily culturally freighted comes the popular culture of postmodernity, with its celebration of difference, of otherness, with its syncretism, nostalgia and playfulness, but also with its weary scepticism and 'post-historical' indifference. It is a culture based on the belief that everything arises within the realm of large-scale human relationships within the world, from within cultures, with no obvious place for God if God is a God remote from the world.

In the next chapter the role of science at the Enlightenment in the removal of God from involvement in the world will be considered. For now, suffice it to say that a closed Newtonian world of 'push me pull you' leaves only limited scope for divine intervention, which in the hands of Laplace and the deists disappeared altogether.[10] The prescientific understanding of God as involved in all of reality and all events is lost, and an only occasionally intervening deity remains, or else the creator who bequeaths to us a self-regulating system prior to withdrawing. But the withdrawn God of the deists might have done a better job of it, just as the still intervening God might intervene more reliably (here are two planks of the protest atheism already mentioned). But before that even, there is doubt about adequate evidence for this remote God. A closed scientific world, in which knowledge emerges reliably only in empirical investigation, is not religiously suggestive. And herewith a particular dimension of atheism these last two hundred and fifty years. It becomes increasingly difficult to connect imaginatively to the idea of God in a universe from which God is remote – banished to the world's edges, for instance, to its beginning and ending, and banished from credibility as an invisible agent for whose presence and action there is little or nothing that can be called 'real evidence'.

To be sure, attempts continue to this day to find God within this scientifically delimited world. One is by arguments from design. William Paley in his widely read *Natural Theology* (1802) invoked an invisible watchmaker to account for the intricacy and apparently carefully crafted nature of the world. Today the argument from design regularly makes use of the so-called 'strong anthropic principle'. This principle states that because of infinitesimally finely tuned fundamental constants of nature, and other uniquely generative features characteristic of fundamental physical reality, all of which we now know to be necessary for the world to be amenable to our presence in it, for life and mind to have ever emerged in our universe, then the world *is* as it is to make our emergence possible. This conclusion has been theologically appropriated as proof of a divine hand at work in setting up such enormously improbable initial conditions.[11]

What are we to make of the argument from design, in its traditional and in its more recent 'strong anthropic' forms? The argument that as the watch suggests a watchmaker, so the even more intricate world-as-a-whole suggests a creator, gives rise to the problem of evil, with which it admittedly has difficulty, as we have seen. But there is another equally telling problem with it. On the grounds that we need not appeal to design to explain the complexity of living things, the argument has a particularly effective opponent in that doggedly naturalistic apostle of radical Darwinism, the evolutionary biologist Richard Dawkins. In one after another compelling book, and with numerous examples from every corner of the plant and animal world, he accounts for the enormous diversity and complexity of evolved life on the basis of what amounts to a simple natural algorithm: given enough time, endless types of creature will evolve under natural selection to exploit their environments optimally, with the gene's all-consuming compulsion toward self-perpetuation providing the vital force. The idea of God somehow guiding this process by design is seen to be superfluous – there is no overarching plan being worked out, but only a welling-up of ever greater diversity by the purely natural action of blind and undirected forces.[12] In Paley's time, when we could still believe in a relatively recent Earth and fixity from the outset of all the animal species living upon it, design was a powerful argument. But the nineteenth century unseated all of that, first with geology and then with biology, while evolutionary biology in the twentieth century has offered a fully naturalistic explanation.

As for the strong anthropic principle, a further naturalistic argument can be made against it. Other universes may have got off the ground before this one, and then promptly collapsed without anything much happening beyond billionths of a second of paltry physics. But given enough emergences and collapses of this sort, it is not inconceivable that randomness will ultimately throw up something decent. And once the physics and chemistry is advanced enough to let the biochemistry and biology get going, later factors will determine what evolves – not the conditions of the initial 'singularity'. The power of evolution to build a teeming world of highly adapted creatures has been demonstrated by Richard Dawkins and others. Given enough time, brains may become complex enough for consciousness to emerge. So perhaps all you need is the right physics to get a viable universe going, after which the chemistry will in time throw up biochemistry, thence in time to life and finally to the evolution of intelligent, conscious life.

I am not suggesting that evolutionary outcomes are inevitable. Life would have evolved differently in different conditions and in response to different events. If the dinosaurs had not been wiped out, for instance, we humans may not have evolved. But there is an argument that life and intelligent life will be limited in the forms it can take. There are advantages in binocular vision, for instance, and in bilateral symmetry – especially if you want to be able to move quickly in a straight line. And there is a range of possible sizes that is difficult for viable life forms to overreach, with microbes and sperm whales indicating its likely limits.[13] But of course such details do not have to be planned in advance. Even though its options are not infinite, nevertheless nature does find a way.

I conclude that we can discern God in this whole process, but that we cannot prove God from it. Randomness and aeons of evolution have given us 'all things bright and beautiful'. Religion has to find other ways of affirming the reality of God, for this particular gap is now closed. As a result this version of the argument from design ultimately collapses into the so-called 'weak anthropic principle', which is the simple recognition that cosmic conditions must be as they are for us to be here at all. That is non-controversial, interesting and wonderful, but it will not underwrite a successful argument from design. The extraordinarily generative fine tunings of physical reality highlighted by the anthropic principle compel attention and even excite the religious imagination, but the principle has not proved apologetically compelling.

Perhaps the weakness of these arguments from design is that once we have got used to thinking of God separated from the world it is difficult to sneak God back in by another route. The willingness to concede divine activity 'in, with and under' scientifically elaborated world processes must await a renewal of God-images. Scepticism today has trouble relating a remote and unrelated God with a fundamentally relational world. And I cannot but conclude that this expression of atheism is based on good theological instincts.

As an alternative to seeking its evidence in natural realms which are increasingly in the hands of scientists, much modern theology has abandoned that particular engagement and taken up the fight on a supposedly more promising front, that of human experience and interiority. And hence a long tradition in Protestant and more recently in Roman Catholic theology seeking signs of God in human moral and religious experience, or else in self-transcending aspects of human thought and action more generally. There are many notable examples of this approach, from Pascal and pietism in the seventeenth century through Kant in the eighteenth and Schleiermacher in the nineteenth century to Protestants like Paul Tillich and Roman Catholics like Karl Rahner in recent decades. But the genie of atheism is now gleefully out of the bottle, with new manifestations of unbelief deemed by many to outdo these newer apologetic strategies, despite their claims to offer more secure arguments for an age of science.

As for such apologetics based on the universal contours of human being, knowing and acting, or perhaps of religious experience, theology faces the postmodern challenge of humanity's significant diversity, and its claim that culture goes 'all the way down' in defining what it is to be human. Such apologetics will gain no purchase without a significantly agreed-upon account of the human condition on which to hang a theology. Nor is the objection that religions can be accounted for as cultural artefacts ever far from reach in the armoury of today's atheism. Religions are regularly dismissed by sceptics as quirky bits of folk culture at best, or pernicious cultural survivals from less enlightened times at worst. Their cultural and social function is seen as sufficient to explain them, without remainder. So religions are not taken seriously, and if seriously then seldom on their own terms.

And who can doubt that religion does regularly collapse into its cultural functions, as the repository and pictorial reinforcement of significant social beliefs, practices and taboos? The Church from the beginning, from as early as the New Testament writings, has struggled against this to articulate and preserve a radical, culturally transforming understanding of its Gospel, in the face of constant pressures toward conservatism, quietism and social conformity. Contrary to these excellent instincts, the Church at its least authentic has provided and continues to provide ammunition for atheistic assessments of religion. Underwhelmed by their experience of the Church and its claims, sceptics regularly categorize religion and belief in God as a purely human construction in response to immature human needs.

The problem here is that as God has been removed from the physical world in an age of science, so too has God become distanced from the human world. And this in at least three ways. First, the increasingly autonomous human person of the modern period has rejected external authority as heteronomous and ignoble. God as an external source of validation or agent of control is not going to be more palatable if reintroduced as an inner reality of religious feeling, or as a necessary component of human functioning, which had so recently and so gladly claimed its independence. Second, the increasing sense in this postmodern period that human beings form part of the web of life in nature means that a God remote from the world is a God equally remote from the human. Gone then is any spiritual affinity there might once have been between a God remote from the world and spiritually elevated creatures made in God's own image themselves understood to be equally remote from the world. Humanity is increasingly conceived in naturalistic terms, as a creature of Earth rather than an exile from heaven. And, third, the postmodern realization that individual human subjectivity is heavily influenced by culture, even accounted for by it, tells against any timeless and other-worldly understanding of even the most elevated human motives and truths. If it all comes from within the human world, which is a part of the natural world, and God is remote from that world, then God is redundant and it is pointless to invoke God in explaining human interiority even at its most spiritual.

Significantly, belief in God survives. Many are unaware of these specific critiques (although they reflect widespread sentiment in the West and not only from educated sceptics). Many others are unmoved by them. Equally, however, many Christians have been helped to reconceive God in ways that allow intellectual and imaginative engagement between faith and the emerging physically, biologically, humanly and culturally relational world-view. The reasons for belief are complex, and hardly reducible to a slick line in apologetics. Nevertheless, today's reimagining of God beyond the remote figure bequeathed to us by the seventeenth century is significant. God's presence and action in the world can now be rethought in conversation with this newly holistic cosmology and anthropology, as we will see in the chapters to follow.

Secularity

The third and final feature of life in the world that we will take note of is secularity, or secularization. This sociological term has various meanings.[14] It points to the decline of Church membership, since the industrial revolution and the large-scale urbanization of the West. It refers to decline in the wealth, prestige and social influence of the churches, which once dominated the cultural, political and even the economic life of Europe. And then there is the severance of religiosity from formal religious observance, which manifests itself in the widespread privatization of religious and spiritual beliefs and practices in the West today, untroubled by separation from communities of faith, canons of orthodoxy and even the demands of reason.

At the level of experience, secularity means that people have internalized the purported remoteness of God from the world. Science accounts for the way things go, and while divine involvement in the world may be a folk memory resurgent in hard times, it is not by and large taken seriously. The way people live indicates that their life is part of a closed world system in which human beings must shoulder all the responsibilities and come up with all the answers. Daily life is lived functionally without God, throughout. So it is by and large with the personalities of public, economic and social life. The legislatures, the courts, the media, the corporations and the stock exchanges help define a world without cosmic resonances or ultimate ends. The West seeks happiness, entertainment, meaning and purpose in the small world of paid work, home and family, children and grandchildren and, of course, 'lifestyle'. Existence is illuminated by the doings of celebrities, televised sport, computer games, internet browsing and an extensive diet of fiction on film, video and television.

To be sure, the longing for something more than material consumption and the fragile contentment of family life remains. The decline of churches is matched by the rise of 'spirituality', an often eclectic affair, with various beliefs and practices from Eastern religions and psychotherapy cobbled together into one or another feral philosophy which 'works for me'. Disciplined allegiance to an authoritative tradition and commitment to a critical conversation between the world and that tradition is out of vogue; organized religion is a shadow of its former self. To be sure, Western society today exhibits much ritual participation, from the sports field to the gym to the nightclub to the holiday resort to the talk show to the inner-city café to the bedroom, but less and less of it involves the churches.

If God appears anywhere today it is as a private matter, a recreational option, a 'part of life', but no longer is God the centre and circumference of meaning and purpose for society as a whole. Not everyone practised their religion in the centuries of Christendom, before secularity grew up in the wake of Enlightenment, but heaven and Earth and the whole human drama were still defined by the stories and background beliefs of religion whether one went to church or not. But today even believers struggle to relate their faith to life in the world. Here again we have the legacy of a remote God, who has been edged out of science and culture's closed and self-sufficient world.

It is not a bad thing that science has emptied the Western world of gods and spirits, so that, for instance, the true causes of disease could be found and the technological exploitation of natural materials and environments begin to improve our human lot. But the flip side of our de-divinized world has been a sense of cosmic aloneness. Existentialists have focused on this for over a century, and twentieth-century Western literature knew all about meaninglessness, emptiness and ennui. The green revolution currently gathering steam in the West, as well as representing an important corrective to the detached exploitation of nature which is no longer sustainable, is also a romantic movement. As Romanticism in the eighteenth century grew up in protest against the spiritually lean culture of scientific rationality, so today the secularized urban Westerner increasingly sees the outdoors and wild nature as a place of spiritual communion. To be sure this was not generally possible before nature was significantly subdued and its often inhospitable otherness made safe for ecotourism – it is hard to be a rural romantic or a nature mystic when survival involves daily struggle with nature. But it is an important indicator that a void in today's Western sensibility remains following the withdrawal of God.

The atheist is of course equally sceptical about today's grab bag of ill-considered quasi-religious beliefs and spiritualities. And while very likely to share in the deep appreciation of natural beauty characteristic of a largely urban culture, the atheist is not going to read anything supernatural into such elevated feelings. The atheist is likely to accept life in all its ordinariness, and savour anything beautiful or wonderful without the intrusion of religion into sentiment. Life's business will be transacted without reference to any higher power, and no inexplicable phenomena will be seen to require a religious explanation. God will not be invoked to account for or justify anything whatever, because God has been defined out of the world. And hence God will not be experienced in the world.

It is important to realize that the remoteness of God is not just a problem for unbelievers. Modern Christians are regularly affected, too. Many drift uneasily on the fringes of belief, habituated to worship perhaps but unable to connect intellectually or imaginatively with the remote God presented in many pulpits and in many a stultifying liturgical backwater.

Some of these are young people whose oft-heard complaint that worship is boring and irrelevant masks a serious desire for a God involved in the traffic of life in the world, rather than impossibly remote from the creative, celebratory, exploratory, bitter-sweet depths that these young people experience. And because the Church is not good at providing what they seek, many will not develop into adult believers – they will either become atheists or else seek a holistic religious vision privately, or in some other forum.

Others live disaffected Christian lives in their middle years, sustained by glimpses of a holistic spirituality in relationships and creative work, in music and the arts, in nature walks and gardening, in the fulfilment of human potential. But these impeccable catholic instincts are often not reflected back to people, celebrated, corrected and fulfilled, in the Church's preaching, teaching, life and worship.

But it need not be this way. Secularity can be anything but religiously neutral for the modern Western believer. Dietrich Bonhoeffer was a powerful witness to the 'secular faith' he saw emerging. Hanged in April 1945 for his involvement with Count Stauffenberg, Admiral Canaris and others in the plot to blow up Hitler, he was until his last months writing hopeful radical theology from a Nazi prison cell. This is the sort of theologian an atheist ought to like.

Rather than a God remote from the world and contemptuous of the world, a God served by life-denying, mealy-mouthed religion; rather than a religion reified and condemned to pious interiority leaving the rest of life cheapened and spiritually denuded, Bonhoeffer traced in the steps of his spiritual forebear Martin Luther the presence of God hidden yet active 'in, with and under' events, in a world which God has given into the responsibility of human beings. This is not a God who will meddle, and dishonour human beings by relieving them of their proper task and identity. Nor is this a God who will make a powerful display to grant religious assurance, preferring instead the powerless anonymity of the crucified one. This is a God who suffers with humanity, who accepts alongside us the incompleteness and ambiguity which have been so searchingly traced in modern Western experience.

Hence Bonhoeffer's paradox of living in the world *etsi deus non daretur*, living before God as if there were no God. Thus a religious existence fully committed to life in the world is commended, without the religious props atheists declare asinine and reject out of hand. Bonhoeffer puts the point famously in a letter of July 1944: 'The God who makes us live in this world without using him as a working hypothesis is the God before whom we are ever standing. Before God and with him we live without God. God allows himself to be edged out of the world and on to the cross.'[15]

While Bonhoeffer was unable to complete his elaboration of this tantalizing thesis, nevertheless subsequent theology has explored themes of God's absence and 'death', striving toward a view of faith and a praxis of Church which honours the ambiguities, inevitabilities and possibilities of life in the world. How the hidden God might be present and act in the world is considered against all the challenges of unbelief we have noted in this chapter – human vulnerability and culpability in a world of overwhelming suffering, a holistic and suggestively self-sufficient scientific account of reality, involving an awareness of cultural forces in determining individual sensibility, and the plain fact that, good or bad, life in our modern secular world is often an experience of God's absence, for unbelievers and for believers alike.

Some important attempts to rethink God in these conditions will be considered in Chapter 3, below. Consequent reflections on what ought and can be said, along with what ought not and can no longer be said about divine action in the world will follow in Chapters 4, 5 and 6. In all of this a major aim will be to ease the burdens that unhelpful images of God have placed on belief since the Enlightenment. But for now it is important to establish and explore more fully the link made in this chapter between God's remoteness from our world and the loss of belief in God.

Notes

1 See a fine sermon by Karl Rahner SJ on this theme, 'Epiphany: the blessed journey of the God-seeking person', in *The Great Church Year: The Best of Karl Rahner's Homilies, Sermons and Meditations* (1987) (New York: Crossroad, 1994), pp. 101–6.

2 Sally Jackson interviewing Robyn Williams, 'Unholy Communion', *The Australian*, 6 January 1999, p. 9.

3 Fyodor Dostoyevsky, *The Brothers Karamazov* (1880) (London: Penguin, 1958/1982), in particular Pt 2, Bk 5, Ch. 4, 'Rebellion', in which the agnostic Ivan inquires of Alyosha 'to torture to death only one tiny creature … and to found the edifice (of human destiny) on her unavenged tears – would you consent to be the architect on those conditions?' (p. 287).

4 Albert Camus, *The Plague* (1947) (London: Penguin, 1960), in particular Pt 4, Ch. 3, in which the tireless but atheistic Dr Rieux protests to Fr Paneloux after an incessantly screaming boy has finally succumbed to plague! 'No, Father. I've a very different idea of love. And until my dying day I shall refuse to love a scheme of things in which children are put to torture' (p. 178).

5 Hans Küng, *Does God Exist?* (1978) (London: Collins, 1980), E.II., pp. 442–77.

6 Maurice Wiles, 'Divine action: some moral considerations', in Thomas F. Tracy (ed.), *The God Who Acts: Philosophical and Theological Explorations* (University Park: Pennsylvania State University Press, 1994), pp. 22–3.

7 On quantum physics see, e.g., John Gribbin, *In Search of Schrödinger's Cat* (New York: Bantam, 1984).

8 For good accounts of this see Steven Weinberg, *The First Three Minutes: A Modern View of the Origin of the Universe* (London: Trinity, 1977), and Stephen Hawking, *A Brief History of Time: From the Big Bang to Black Holes* (New York: Bantam, 1988).

9 Chaos is helpfully introduced in James Gleick, *Chaos: Making a New Science* (London: Cardinal, 1988), and Ian Stewart, *Does God Play Dice? The New Mathematics of Chaos* (London: Penguin, 1990).

10 For deism and the science/religion issue see James Byrne, *Glory, Jest and Riddle: Religious Thought in the Enlightenment* (London: SCM, 1996), Chs 5 and 7.

11 On the principle in its various forms see John D. Barrow and Frank J. Tipler, *The Anthropic Cosmological Principle* (Oxford: Oxford University Press, 1986). On the argument from design employing the anthropic principle see Stephen T. Davis, *God, Reason and Theistic Proofs* (Grand Rapids, MI: Eerdmans, 1997), pp. 107–15; see also Mark William Worthing, *God, Creation and Contemporary Physics* (Minneapolis, MN: Fortress, 1996), pp. 43–7.

12 Richard Dawkins, *The Selfish Gene* (Oxford: Oxford University Press, 1976; 2nd edn 1989); *The Blind Watchmaker: Why the Evidence of Evolution Reveals a Universe Without Design* (New York: Norton, 1986).

13 For a fascinating discussion of this matter see John D. Barrow in a less anthropic mood in *The Artful Universe* (Oxford: Clarendon, 1996).

14 See, e.g., Anthony Giddens, *Sociology* (Cambridge: Polity, 1989), pp. 476–8; also Bryan Wilson, *Religion in a Secular Society: A Sociological Comment* (London: Penguin, 1966).

15 Dietrich Bonhoeffer, *Letters and Papers from Prison* (New York: Macmillan, 1953), p. 219.

2 Theism and Atheism

Religion, with all of its intersubjectivities, cannot but be destroyed if dissolved into some other human experience in order to justify its most critical cognitive claims. Eventually such a dissolution will out as atheism.

Michael J. Buckley, SJ
At the Origins of Modern Atheism, 1987

The delicate web of relationships that is at the core of the Jewish-Christian tradition, holding the living God, humanity, and the world together in harmony, was broken, and Western Christianity had produced its own alienation.

Frans Josef van Beeck, SJ
God Encountered (Vol. 2, Pt II), 1994

... nonsense for nonsense, I like the Jesuits better than the philosophes.

Horace Walpole
Letter to George Selwyn, 2 December 1765

Everywhere Christian theism is in question, deemed by both unbelievers and believers alike to dehumanize, alienate and intellectually embarrass. As part of the 1960s' ferment a South London bishop, in what turned out to be a million-plus best-seller,[1] popularized Paul Tillich's redefinition of God as the 'Ground of Being', 'the beyond in the midst', declaring the remote 'theistic' notion of a God 'out there' to be unhelpful and unchristian. Recently another Anglican bishop has revisited the same issue, rejecting the God of Christian tradition as an invasive superperson and, what is more, a human projection. From the variety of projection theories underpinning humanistic atheism, the one he lit upon was that of Sigmund Freud, that God emerged at the same time as human consciousness as a necessary expedient for calming our nerves once we discovered aloneness and responsibility.[2] So Christian theism has become uncomfortable even for bishops! It is taken to imply remoteness from the world and from life on God's part, and to invite charges of atheism.

It is the contention of this chapter and the next that the God being rejected here, the God who has indeed spawned modern and postmodern forms of atheism, is not what Christianity really means by God. The next chapter will look at the traditions of the Church and find a God who is anything but remote from the world, indifferent to suffering or disconnected from the human. In panentheistic but also in 'plain Trinitarian' reflection a very different God will emerge from the one regularly deemed to be the enemy of human knowledge and emancipation. In this chapter a start will be made by considering how God came to be understood as remote from the world and from human experience, and hence ripe for the atheistic picking.

The first part of this chapter will seek to clarify the form of Christian theistic belief increasingly deemed to be problematic. 'Classical theism' is identified as existing in some tension with the demands Christian faith makes of God-talk. Viewed from both its speculative and ideological functions the adequacy and appropriateness of classical theism is called into question.

The second part of this chapter will look at how emerging scientific ways of thinking led theology to overemphasize the God of classical theism at the expense of more holistic images from the Bible and the tradition. In this we will need to pursue themes in the history of ideas through the Enlightenment. I am indebted here to recent revisionist history which insists that the tradition of Christian God-talk is not fundamentally distorted, but that it has become distorted since the seventeenth century. The atheism which resulted, which we can for convenience call 'modern atheism', took root because God had been taken out of the world, both natural and human.

In the third part of this chapter we look at how Christian thought responded by seeking to establish belief in God from a starting point within the human self, withdrawing to the fall-back position of interiority once God had been evacuated from the exterior world. This inflation of the self, which is the characteristic strategy of modernity from the Enlightenment well into the nineteenth century, has for some time been under question from postmodern writers. And with the death of the self comes death for the God whose existence was established with reference to that self.

Classical theism

Classical theism is defined as 'belief in the one God, the creator, who is infinite, self-existent, incorporeal, eternal, immutable, impassible, simple, perfect, omniscient and omnipotent'.[3] According to H. P. Owen this sort of language is an inevitable second-order reflection on the living God of the Bible, progressively elaborated for the philosophical environment Christianity encountered in the Graeco-Roman world from the second century.[4] The high points came with Augustine of Hippo in the fourth and fifth centuries and in particular with Thomas Aquinas in the thirteenth.

Owen favours retention of classical theism as the best possible model of God, convinced that its essence is not dry speculation. Thus he attempts to answer a major criticism of classical theism: that its God is remote from the Judaeo-Christian tradition of passionate divine involvement with the world.

So, for instance, Owen allows that while insisting on impassability and omniscience, theists may differ on the attribution of feelings to God, and that while retaining God's all-knowingness, he nevertheless allows that theists may differ on what kinds of things can be known[5] (here one suspects concerns of the process theologians are in view, about difficulties connected with God knowing the future). Frans Josef van Beeck also makes a case for divine *apatheia*, which he insists is not about Stoic mastery of the passions nor does it imply remote impassive indifference. Instead, Christian tradition has bent Stoic and Neoplatonic uses of *apatheia* to express biblical faith in the asymmetry of God's involvement with the world – that it is in no way a compelled nor a reactive involvement, but proceeds freely and graciously from God's very nature. For van Beeck God is not moved from inaction to action by pity, nor does God make magnanimous concessions to the world from a position of far-off detachment. Rather, use of *apatheia* highlights the sovereign freedom of the love which God in fact constantly manifests.[6]

'Philosophical theism is bound to seem barren if it is severed from its roots in religious experience,' Owen admits, 'but it cannot be so severed by the truly Christian theist. The God on whom he speculates is "the living God" whom he knows and worships as the Father of Jesus Christ.'[7] Such special pleading demonstrates, however, that without sustained reinterpretation of philosophical usage, with reference to the sacred narratives of Jewish and Christian faith, classical theism will not as Owen hopes be 'truly Christian'. In this context we consider two main areas of concern over classical theism. One I will call the 'speculative captivity of theism' and the other the 'ideological captivity of theism'.

The 'speculative captivity of theism'

To assert 'the speculative captivity of theism' is to assert that despite the goodwill of its defenders, classical theism is fatally mired in imagery of divine aloofness and detachment. In the next chapter we will consider more hopeful models for doing justice to the God of Christian faith and witness. John Macquarrie calls these various options 'dialectical theism'; others among the process theologians have called them 'dipolar theism'. In both cases the emphasis is on achieving the right mix between divine transcendence and immanence. For now we note concerns Macquarrie expresses about classical theism.[8]

There is the prominence of God as creator according to a certain reading of Thomas Aquinas' famous 'five ways'. The God who emerges as 'first cause', 'unmoved mover', etc. is not a God who can readily be understood as involved in the world thus created. More generally the understanding of creation implied here is that it takes place from 'outside' the world. Moreover, there is an arbitrariness about it that does not foster a sense of God's commitment to the world. Macquarrie here recognizes an invitation in

Christian theology for deism and atheism. We will see that this reading of Thomas Aquinas is not fair to his subtle position, but it does reflect the unfortunate process whereby the saint has been turned into a rationalist. But more of this shortly.

Then there is the problem of conceiving God's action in the world if God is seen to be remote. The traditional understanding of divine action, whereby secondary causes mediate the primary activity of God, will be examined in Chapter 4, below. It is an approach intended to give the world its due in directing its own affairs, while recognizing that God is behind it all and can still perform special acts as well as act uniformly. But such action becomes a problem for theology and philosophy if God is understood to be outside the world, intruding into the closed weave of the world's own processes – to act is to 'intervene'. 'If we could understand the world-process as more closely integrated into the being of God,' however, Macquarrie concludes that 'then it might be possible to reconceive the belief that God acts in the world.'[9]

Finally there is the burden of divine impassability. Creative reinterpretations such as that of van Beeck show that this is only a serviceable religious idea for Christian faith if it is very nearly inverted, and turned into an image about the true nature of divine passion for the life of the world. For his part Macquarrie is concerned about the risk of devaluing the cosmos inherent in assertions of impassability, that the world has no effect on God. Later in the chapter we will see that to devalue the cosmos in this way is to court atheism. Macquarrie is also troubled by the image of a static, timeless and immutable God which ensues – self-contained, aloof, frozen. Which leads us naturally into a further area of debate, in which we are alerted to the ideological alliances served by a static, aloof deity.

The 'ideological captivity of theism'

To assert 'the ideological captivity of theism' is to assert that the God of classical theism is politically implicated. Perhaps it need not be this way. Perhaps the God of classical theism, so unlike anything in the world, so transcending normal categories, can serve as a corrective to the imprisonment of God in one or another religious straitjacket, one or another tribal allegiance. Classical theism can thus be understood as a protest movement against other forms of God's ideological captivity.[10] But one can argue that just the opposite is also the case, that a corrective can in time demand its own correction. And so it is with classical theism, which has itself become ideologically freighted.

The protest atheism and the deconstruction of oppressive narratives discussed in Chapter 1, above, point to just such moral and political encumbrances. The remote, all-powerful, intervening deity of classical theism, entire in himself, has served as an ideology of power writ large. He has sat at the pinnacle of a world in which much dehumanizing suffering is regularly meted out to innocent victims in the name of preserving powers and hierarchies, yet God's all-seeing and all-knowing perspective somehow sanitizes this and makes it all right. Thus God functions as a symbol of dominant values in society, and a justification for their enforcement. This God is not a God who bucks the system and inverts the status quo, which we regularly see happening in the Gospels when Jesus has his turn at shaping God-talk. Modern thought, from the emphasis on human autonomy in Kant through to its atheistic assertion in Marx, Nietzsche and Freud, has seen this one, controlling God as the enemy of human freedom and dignity. 'Rightly or wrongly,' Colin Gunton points out, 'a deity whose oneness is stressed is commonly associated with totalitarian or repressive forms of social order.'[11] A further atheistic critique is that this particular image of God is a human projection. The humanistic cause of the nineteenth and twentieth centuries, borne by such important figures as Feuerbach, Durkheim, Marx and Freud, involved the identification of this God as a projection of human ideals, social values, economic arrangements or immature wishes.[12] Emancipation and maturity for the human race thus came to be linked to emancipation from belief in this God.

A new perspective on this issue is provided by feminist theology. The remote, all-powerful, unbending God is seen not only to be a human projection but in particular a masculine projection, an earthly patriarch gone metaphysical, unable to relate properly, to feel, suffer or change. 'A feminist perspective that prizes mutuality in relations quickly parts company with classical theism,' responds Elizabeth Johnson, 'critiquing its isolationist and dualist patterns.'[13] Commenting on the ideological function served by classical theism, Johnson maintains that 'it is not accidental that classical theism insists on a concept of God with no real relation to the world, even when this is interpreted as an affirmation of divine transcendence. Unrelated and unaffected by the world, such a theistic God limns the ultimate patriarchal ideal, the solitary, dominant male.'[14] So while Owen is confident that with the right Christian handling, the speculations of classical theism will serve the cause of genuinely Christian God-talk, the 'ideological captivity of theism' points to the temptations inherent in the speculative path he advocates.

Separating God from the world

Our investigation of the roots of atheism in *seventeenth*-century theology begins by noting the environment in which the early *sixteenth*-century Church found itself. The Reformation had taken place and the map of Europe had been redrawn. Religious wars fought along confessional lines had caused much bloodshed, and religious sanction was regularly used in the suppression of free thought and dissent. Religious differences had political consequences in a pre-modern world where the stability of states required conformity of belief. So when Europe became full of religious divisions, there were pressures to find new bases for agreement. Classical culture and science provided significant opportunities.

Hence, part of the intellectual environment in which theology worked was the recovery of classical literature and learning in the Renaissance. The atheists of classical antiquity began receiving theological attention, though not as we shall see in a fully theological way. From its stirrings in medieval nominalism science was also growing toward its eighteenth-century arrival as the chief arbiter of meaning and even of value in the West. It was in this context that the theology of Thomas Aquinas began to be rethought, and our path to theology becoming easy prey for atheism began its two-hundred-year course.

The philosophizing of God

The Dominican Thomas de Vio (1469–1534), who in his later role as Master General of the Order and known as Cardinal Cajetan was a dialogue partner with Luther, had begun late in the fifteenth century to systematize Aquinas' doctrine of analogy. He argued for enhanced access to God on the basis of human perceptions, beyond the equivocation Aquinas saw as a necessary part of God-talk. But it was with the Jesuit Francisco Suarez (1548–1617) that Aquinas became what most Protestant and Roman Catholic theology has subsequently taught, a champion of human access to the existence of God by philosophical reflection alone, and to God's attributes by proportional analogy with human attributes. Following Duns Scotus (not Aquinas), Suarez saw the being of God and of creatures as of the same sort, opening what Jean-Luc Marion called a 'univocist drift' in the way God was garnered to human philosophical reckoning – the beginning in history of what William Placher memorably calls 'the domestication of transcendence'.[15]

Placher traces the effect of this thinking on subsequent Protestant thought, making much of the very 'un-Reformation' way in which Protestant Scholasticism in the seventeenth century took up analogical ways of relating the human to the divine directly from Father Suarez. Both the Lutheran Andreas Quenstedt and the Calvinist Francis Turretin are demonstrated to be followers of Aquinas as reinterpreted by Suarez, while the Calvinist Girolamo Zanchi allows that, while the Bible tells us about God, philosophy is what we use to understand the biblical terms.[16] But it is the influence of this trend on Roman Catholic thinkers that carries our account forward.

Another Jesuit, a Dutch student of Suarez, brought this emphasis to bear on the debate with the atheism of classical antiquity. Leonhard Lessius (1554–1623) entered the lists by opposing the atheists of antiquity with their own philosophical means. There was also a sense that religious disputes had rendered recourse to dogmatic certainties unusable in commending the faith. So something more neutral was sought, apart from reference to God in Christ, or the work of the Spirit in fostering faith, since so much blood as well as ink had so recently been spilled over such issues. Aquinas was read piecemeal, as has so often been the case subsequently, and his cosmological arguments used to find evidence for God in the world, following the lead of Cicero and Stoicism.

A French contemporary, a first-rate mathematician and correspondent with leading scientists of the day, took a similar line, albeit one influenced by Plato and Epicurean philosophy, identifying the creator of the world from Genesis with the mover of the Cosmos in Aristotle in a synthesis where God becomes the explanation of all phenomena. Like the Jesuit Lessius, this brilliant Minim Father, Marin Mersenne (1588–1648), was also influenced by the rising tide of pietism, whereby religious practice and experience was being separated from the philosophical prosecution of God-talk. This trend marked both Dutch and French Church life. It is a terrible irony that France in the subsequent centuries produced such significant exploration of the spiritual life in figures from Pascal to Berulle to the Curé d'Ars while at the same time French philosophy overwhelmed what religious sensibility remained in the Enlightenment, with its establishment of modern atheism. But we are ahead of ourselves. Only in an extraordinary figure like Blaise Pascal (1623–1662) were the insights of dawning science and the religious impulses of the tradition kept in harmony. For the likes of Fathers Lessius and Mersenne, however, as Michael Buckley points out with some incredulity, 'it is as if sixteen hundred years of religious history had never occurred.'[17]

Buckley is clearly pained by the omissions of his Jesuit forebear Lessius, indeed by the whole turn, whereby 'impersonal nature was made the primary warrant for a profoundly personal Christian God.'[18] His eloquent lament deserves to be quoted in full.

The Christian culture of Europe within which these theological apologetics were launched incarnated a sense of divinity which was both intimately personal and present, a god whose tangible religious atmosphere could be found in the village churches and local monasteries as well as with the crucifix on the walls of taverns and the great celebrations which punctuated the year, a god whose interventions were the stuff of prayer and mysticism, ritual and rural superstition. This transcendence was woven into the texture of the culture and Christ defined the meaning and the truth about god. Daily patterns of speech bespoke this permeating influence, and the success or failure of life was judged by it. Precisely this determination of life as a whole precluded a fundamental return to the Stoic and Epicurean philosophies. The providential *numen* and the sovereign architect lay at too great a distance from what this religious culture recognised as god, against whom a putative atheism was deemed to be antagonistic. The determinations of

Lessius and Mersenne abstracted God from Christ as either definition or manifestation. The Christian god was to be justified without Christ.[19]

This image of a God as anything but remote from the world, human life and today's spiritual yearnings will be taken up more fully in Chapter 3, below. For now we follow the trail of emerging theological grounds for the eventual denial of this newly remote God with the impact of Lessius and Mersenne.

The way of reading Aquinas advocated by Suarez was absorbed by René Descartes (1596–1650), and he was led further along in this direction by the influence of Lessius and Mersenne. Descartes' attempt to find absolutely certain knowledge in the midst of his fluid and changing century made him look to God as guarantor of the intelligibility of the world. In a different place and at a slightly later time, a different man with a different religion was also feeling the effect of Lessius. Isaac Newton (1642–1727) knew of Lessius because his writings had been popularized in England (and this by Sir Walter Raleigh!). Newton's emerging universal mechanics would not work properly without the intervention of God to correct drift in planetary orbits. And in the images of God emerging from Lessius and Mersenne a sufficiently instrumental God became available, suitable for physical and metaphysical use. Like Stephen Hawking today, following on in a direct cultural line, the scientifically minded Descartes and Newton 'registered their recognition of the theological office fallen to them'.[20]

The influence of this growing tradition was felt in England by the priest Samuel Clarke (1675–1729) and in France by the priest Nicolas Malebranche (1638–1715). Both arrived at a fundamental tension between God and the world of matter. Clarke denied revealed religion and argued that God could be known by inference from behind a world of matter, seen as thin stuff – as atoms bumping regularly about in a void of non-being. Malebranche so separated the realms of mind and matter bequeathed to him by Descartes that he allowed no capacities, no causative abilities, to the material world at all, insisting that everything in the world was moved and actualized and caused by God directly, denying secondary causes. They both linked their glorification of God with the denigration of matter, and as Buckley observes with characteristic élan, 'The time was soon to come when this despised matter would wreak a terrible revenge on both theologians and their god. Christology, with its doctrine of the Incarnation, would have read matter religiously in a very different manner.'[21]

The rejection of God

And so it was. It is not fair to say that the Enlightenment was a time of atheism, although there was much criticism of the Church and its pretensions in France and there were philosophes who lived in the twilight of deism rather than the night of atheism. But with the great encyclopaedist Denis Diderot (1713–1784) a dynamic naturalism emerged that did dispense with God. His infamous *Letter on the Blind* (1749) has its hero, the blind mathematician Saunderson, expire with the words 'O thou God of Clarke and Newton, have mercy on me', after advising a friend simply to accept a materialistic world and not seek a divine explanation for it.[22] From Descartes, Diderot takes the dynamic nature of matter, but not the God invoked to undergird it metaphysically. From Newton he takes the law-driven physical universe, but not the God that propped it up. 'Diderot's Saunderson introduces a critical transition in western thought with his dismissal of transcendence and assertion of dynamic matter' concludes Buckley. 'He introduces atheism.'[23]

And this was the emerging mood in all areas of natural and biological science at the time. The Swiss zoologist Tremblay had shown that a bisected hydra would regenerate, demonstrating its life essence was within itself. The English Roman Catholic priest Needham had shown micro-organisms and worms would generate in putrefying matter, oversimply (but influentially) concluding that matter gave rise to life.[24] In this same vein, the physician and provocateur Julien LaMettrie (1709–1751) had advanced to the idea that living things could be accounted for purely materialistically, their souls being part of their matter.[25]

But where the encyclopaedist Diderot had significantly advanced this trend, it fell to a wealthy long-term German resident of Paris, Baron Paul d'Holbach (1723–1789), to complete a totally atheistic and materialistic system of thought so advanced that even the deist Voltaire rejected it and its proposal of 'thinking matter' as scandalous. *The System of Nature* (1770), d'Holbach's great achievement, set the natural world free from any external cause, naturalized and organicized animal and human life without remainder and accounted for the ethical (another great Enlightenment preoccupation) purely in terms of what is useful.

So climaxed a process whereby philosophy generated an independent mechanical and organic world, and only temporarily had need of God as an explanation. The theists Lessius and Mersenne, Descartes and Newton, Clarke and Malebranche, had left a fundamentally non-religious but theoretically necessary theism which in a more scientifically confident century was deemed to be otiose – as unnecessary as claims of revelation and authority on the part of the Church were deemed to be offensive. A new and virulent atheism was released. A God defined by theology to be remote from the world, from human experience, intuition and religious sensibility, had vanished over the horizon altogether. And all because no theological alternative was sought closer to the real wellsprings of lived experience, Trinitarian conviction, doxological faith and prayerful spirituality. What remained was a closed materialism of the public world and at best an irrational religion of the private world.

It is to that private world of the self that we now turn, and to the grand metaphysics erected upon its foundation. Could the self provide firmer support to the God knocked over by Diderot and d'Holbach?

The self and its God

Where does the modern self emerge? Some point to Augustine and his *Confessions*, in which a recognizably modern self-consciousness is evident. Others look to the Middle Ages, to William of Ockham and the rise of nominalism – a philosophical perspective focused on particular things rather than abstract essences, which opened the way to replacing a unifying God with a unifying self.[26] Some would point to the Reformation, with its premium on personal salvation and attention to the spiritual needs of the individual. But others look a century later, to the period after the disruptive and distressing confessional wars of the early seventeenth century when pietism emerged as a major religious movement. Focus on the pious self rather than objective issues of belief and theology strikes William Placher as a major departure from the objectivity of the Reformation, which was focused on the Gospel rather than the self; 'the greatest documents of the Reformation are its biblical commentaries,' Placher notes, whereas 'the greatest documents of seventeenth-century Christianity are its diaries and spiritual biographies.'[27] As for beliefs and theologies in their various manifestations, these became distinct compartmentalized things called 'religions', separated in the seventeenth century from the rest of life.[28] This represents the onset of secularization, in which God-talk moved out of the public into the private arena. This process was aided by the emerging middle classes and a bourgeois life based on personal activity in the realm of commerce, whereby the West began to find a workable structure apart from God, attending to the self and its doings.[29]

The rise of the self

The self emerged to philosophical prominence as the certain starting point of knowledge with René Descartes. But it was a more modest thinking self than the one 'discovered' by Jean-Jacques Rousseau (1712–1778), who is credited by Robert Solomon as the first proponent of the modern self in all its universal grandeur, the shared inner aspect of all humanity which the Enlightenment thinkers of Europe variously discerned within. Solomon, with an assessment of Rousseau every bit as dismissive as his assessment of the modern self, finds it 'suggestive that the transcendental pretence was discovered by a sociopath'.[30] But from Rousseau and his influence the fortunes of this self, and the basis for belief in God that it fostered, can be traced.

Immanuel Kant (1724–1804) wrought the greatest revolution in Western thought by shifting meaning from the external 'noumenal' world, where it had hitherto been sought, into the ordering power of the human mind, which imposed order and meaning on the world by its own a priori structures (that we impose rather than observe causality is Kant's best-known example of this). It is these 'phenomenal' ideas we know, not things in the 'noumenal' world, in the fundamental Kantian disjunction of self and world. The self in question is a universal human reality knowable to the individual by introspection. God for Kant is invoked not as the guarantor of a metaphysical system, as for Descartes, nor as a corrective to wobbles in the physics of universal gravitation, as in Newton, nor indeed with any place in 'pure reason'. Rather, Kant's God is a postulate of practical reason, required to exist by the demand of accounting for the self. God for Kant assures that the self in doing its duty will not be forever deprived of the happiness which duty alone does not guarantee, and here is where God comes in – as a necessary part of the drama of an ethical self expecting its dutifulness to be rewarded. This Kantian 'transendental ego' was radicalized by Johann Fichte (1762–1814), who denied the noumenal world altogether in favour of the acting self making the world.

An alternative perspective is offered by the extraordinarily influential German theologian Friedrich Schleiermacher (1768–1834). This self-professed 'pietist of a higher order' was also influenced by the Romantic rejection of dogma and speculation in his attention to the innermost reality of human consciousness. Here he found his site of utmost theological disclosure. Not in any reduction of religion to morality or claims for God as the guarantor of a satisfying moral world, as in Kant, but in the deep unity of intuition and feeling he perceived within, of self and God known together. Schleiermacher did not simply attend to human religious experience, but to a dimension he believed was present in all experience. At bottom, human receptivity discloses a fundamental state of dependence which is absolute, and it is this foundational feeling accessed through reflection that Schleiermacher declares to be our knowledge of God. Famously, Schleiermacher proclaims Jesus as the highest instance of this purely human God-consciousness. A whole tradition of Protestant theologians follows Schleiermacher along this path, with Paul Tillich as a leading modern example. Following Maurice Blondel, Roman Catholic thought has also sought firm knowledge of God in the religious disclosivity of human interiority, with Karl Rahner as the twentieth century's leading exponent of 'transcendental anthropology'. These powerful techniques disclose a lot about the human condition, but they are as prone as Kant's theory of a transcendental ego to dissolution in the acid of cultural relativism. If morality is culturally determined, then what of Kant's categorical imperative? If human experience is not uniform but rather culturally and linguistically determined, then what of Schleiermacher's feeling of absolute dependence? But more of this when we come to the postmoderns. For now, we continue our tracing of this development with the grand attempts of German idealism to link the human self with no less than the universal unfolding of historical purpose.

A more holistic and romantically inspired version of Kant's transcendental ego is offered by Friedrich Schelling (1775–1854), who saw the self as one pole of reality, a 'world soul' opposite nature, and the voice through which the world process came to conscious expression. His Tübingen roommate G. W. F. Hegel (1770–1831) built on this idea and virtually redefined God in terms of the self. Not the individual self, which is a product of the world process, but the self as no less than the mind or spirit of the world process itself, labouring toward full expression through the dialectical back-and-forward of intellectual history. With this comes a new insight much relied upon by the postmodern descendants of Hegel, and that is the recognition of distinct conceptual realities, which rise and fall through history as the argument moves on, with the absolute never to be found among them fully realized. In Hegel the self becomes linked to historical progress and to the high hopes he and many others held for Europe and for German nationalism, all seen as higher evolutions of the human journey. History was to disappoint him.

The fall of the self

This divine self was subsequently much ridiculed and denied, and as Hegel's self met rejection, it dragged divinity down with it. A good example of this is in the upturning of Hegel achieved by the 'young left' Hegelians, Ludwig Feuerbach (1804–1872) and Karl Marx (1818–1883). Feuerbach was a young firebrand when he asserted materialism at the expense of the idealism Hegel had taught him. Instead of individual human beings manifesting in their various ways through history the progress of the divine/human self coming to expression, the opposite was in fact the case – the divine is a projection of the ideals of human individuals; the grand idealistic self is only the individual self writ large. Marx's ideology critique of unjust economic conditions and their religious self-justification was another instance of the reversal of Hegel we first see in Feuerbach. Instead of cultural, economic and political systems being manifestations of the universal spirit grasping the masses, Marx saw the masses producing and maintaining the ideology which oppressed them, and in this they were supported by religion. It was not that history and the God of history produced social and economic conditions, but that social and economic conditions produced history, and the God of history. Free the masses, seize history by revolution and the God of history passes into history.

A passionate opponent of Hegel's system was the melancholy Dane Søren Kierkegaard (1813–1855), who rejected the idealist picture of a grand super-self finding expression in individuals, and using them in the advancing march of the absolute through history. Kierkegaard is called an existentialist because, apart from any such metaphysical determinants of human being, he believed it was up to each individual to choose in order to become fully human. Kierkegaard hated bourgeois Christian conformity and lukewarm faith, asserting the need for individuals to escape the pull of the herd. Nor did he think much of Kant's confidence in the natively dutiful and ethical self assured of its final reward. Kierkegaard understood the authentically human life in terms of relentless struggle through choice, apart from any certainty. There is no God as part of the system for Kierkegaard the radical Christian, but only a mystery grasped in faith through constant recommitment. The grand Western self thus experiences one of its biggest setbacks, and the God joined to it loses foundations. Kierkegaard is an early example of the non-foundational approach to Christian faith later championed by Karl Barth in conscious succession to him. God without the transcendent Western self to cling to becomes a matter of unprovable, 'unnecessary' faith, which is how God appears in the neoconservative and postliberal expressions of post-modern Christianity today – as a self-authenticating but otherwise non-foundational reality known within the language game of Christian life, prayer and worship. But without the props of the modern self, let alone modern science, this God is not publicly meaningful.

The sense of historical diversity and relativism which Hegel introduced was deepened by historicism in the nineteenth century, in particular by Wilhelm Dilthey (1833–1911). He rejected Hegel's absolute end point while keeping Kant's sense that humans make meaning of what they see – in this case by fellow feeling with those they study. Here is a relativist with no absolutes, and no place for the God which Kant and Hegel variously incorporated into their systems. But it was with Friedrich Nietzsche (1844–1900) that the seeds of Hegel's relativism and historicism were most fully radicalized at the expense of the theology inherent in his idealism. Nietzsche disliked the grand idealist systems, thinking them remote from the heroic struggle of life to rise above itself. At the same time he asserted that the objectivity of such systems masked their true character, which was individual and perspectival. Nietzsche applies this same relativism to the absolute morality of Kant, undermining it with a genealogy of morals and an insistence, against Kant's 'categorical imperative', that not everyone is of equal calibre in responding to the demands of morality. And without this absolute morality the Kantian God vanishes. This God is also associated with an insufferably slavish morality built on resentment of the strong and the untroubled, according to Nietzsche, above which humanity must rise. The human end Nietzsche prizes is that of the 'overman', toward whom we journey when we live life with vigour and titanic creative energy. Apartfrom this there is no self, nor any God to support any metaphysical system that will make it easy for us or make certain the outcome. Solomon argues that Nietzsche is not a nihilist, but rather a commentator on the nihilism that emerges when the Kantian and Hegelian ideals are shown up as failures by bourgeois nineteenth-century life, with its lack of robust values and heroic dignity.[31] In Nietzsche we see the complete failure of the grand self, and the rejection of the God it brought with it. The self is something that has to be realized, and for that Nietzsche did not need God. He had his own heroic will and the dream of the 'overman'.

What would happen if you were to take an altogether darker view of the absolute self, keeping it but not the God Kant associated with it nor the positivity Hegel ascribed to it? This is what we see in Arthur Schopenhauer (1788–1860), the philosopher (we might say) of 'the dark side of the force'. His meaningless world, going nowhere, is a prey to absolute will, as is our individual will (over which we have no control), and the whole thing is brutal and directionless. Sexuality is important to Schopenhauer as an illustration of the pointlessness of it all – something that promises happiness is regularly the scourge of happiness. To be sure, this is an instance of perspectivalism, looking on the same world as Kant and Hegel and coming up with an altogether darker, non-theistic view of the absolute self. Significantly, Schopenhauer is the first Western philosopher to be heavily indebted to Eastern religious philosophy, employing the Buddhist critique of desire and its understanding of the self as illusory. Thus God is no necessary concomitant to belief in an absolute self, and that self 'itself' is radically undermined.

Schopenhauer is of interest here not only for himself, but for his influence on Sigmund Freud (1856–1939). The transcendental ego of Kant became for Freud the libidinous 'Id' against which the human has to strive, crafting a rational ego with the aid of Kant's 'categorical imperative', which Freud saw internalized as the 'superego'.[32] The self as good and moral was demolished at the hands of Freud's conflicted and immature modern individual, and the God which went with the self in Kant's system became an immature projection of Freud's unconscious Id – the good self of Kant, rendered dark and destructive by Schopenhauer, brought with it in the form of Freud's unconscious a dispensable parody of Kant's God (and of course Kant's God is a parody of the real Christian God – a God which, by the way, few Christian apologists discern in Freud's parody of the wish-fulfilling, divine Father figure).

The collapse of the modern Western self owes much to Ludwig Wittgenstein (1889–1951), who sought meaning not in any ideal self manifested in individuals but in the public world of language, where meanings are given in use. The self is evident on the surface of life, as it is lived, but not behind life in some idealist metaphysical 'back room of reality'. The radical critique of metaphysical 'behindness' represented by Wittgenstein is typically listed among the telling attacks of postmodernity on the metaphysical tradition of the West, and its association since Plato of God with being. While earlier in this chapter we saw that Aquinas was not the one who championed such a conscripting of God to support a metaphysical system, but rather later

Thomists such as Francisco Suarez and a whole tradition of philosophy he influenced, nevertheless the belief is widespread that theology associates being with God, so that any critique of metaphysics is a critique of God. And Wittgenstein certainly advocated a typically postmodern search for meaning on the surface of life, rather than in its metaphysical basis. The association of God with the modern self, which we have been reviewing, became harder to sustain once Wittgenstein denied that self any identity beyond the to-and-fro of language in ordinary life.

This emphasis on life in the world is also characteristic of Martin Heidegger (1889–1976), who rejected any dualism of self and world in favour of 'being there', *Dasein*, a category he used to name the embeddedness of humanity in reality. *Dasein* is bigger than human individuality and in this sense recalls the modern self of German idealism, and it has contours that can be identified through reflection on life in the world and with others. But Heidegger's individual, like that of Kierkegaard and Sartre, must strive to live authentically, as nothing is given. This becomes increasingly the case for the later Heidegger, who becomes less sure of direct access to being through *Dasein* and more concerned about the limits of what can be named in language. A fertile field for theologians, Heidegger's work inspired constructive reflection on the possible religious disclosivity of experience in the early days (Rahner and Tillich), and atheistic mystical reflections from his later period (in the very latest books of Don Cupitt). The French existentialists of the mid-twentieth century, Jean-Paul Sartre, Albert Camus and Simone de Beauvoir, had no truck with the transcendental self nor with any God attached to it. Simone de Beauvoir emphasized the innate masculineness of this self, and as Solomon observes of this feminist critique of the self and its claims, 'once we have acknowledged this one major split in the idea of humanity, it will be difficult to deny any number of others.'[33]

A last attempt to save the modern self was the structuralism of Claude Levi-Strauss (1908–   ) who modestly claimed that culturally invariant features of humanness were derivable from examination of universal concerns. Certain key distinctions (e.g. between 'raw' and 'cooked') are universal, and disclose fundamental human preoccupations. But this thin self is a shadow of Kant's transcendental ego and Hegel's *Geist*. The poststructuralist revolution of postmodern philosophy, however, subjected this last-ditch effort to save the modern self to intense criticism.

The universal humanness of Levi-Strauss was denied by the radical historicism of Michel Foucault (1926–1984) who showed in a variety of studies that many significant definitions are historically discontinuous and often related to power relations in society. The definition of madness is a good example, and Foucault is relentless in his portrayal of how its meaning has changed and who the definitions have served. Instead of a universal humanity, Foucault's Marxist vision gives us a picture of culture and social power creating human selves.

Jacques Derrida (1930–) is a different but equally important post-modern writer who takes issue with the structuralists in linguistics, arguing essentially that the self and God are examples of a myth of presence upon which Western philosophy has been based, but which is really only an epiphenomenon of language. Language looks so serious and referential, and suggests that it links us to something solid (words like 'presence', 'subject', 'object', 'consciousness'). But language is just sounds, and writing reflects the bias of authors, all of which Derrida brings to the surface through the systematic debunking of metaphysics which is 'deconstruction'. God as the projection of language, and the modern self too, with even individuals being cultural products, is the radicalizing of Marx and the plain death of a whole tradition of the modern self going back to Kant and Rousseau.

Derrida has his theological interpreters, who say that he is a mystic, with a Jewish Kabbalistic sense of a God beyond any God conceivable by human reason. Some even welcome such radical postmodern conclusions, satisfied that beyond the death of God as the shadow of Western metaphysics God can at last be God – as David Tracy puts it, 'the most characteristically postmodern forms of God-talk have allowed the awe-some reality of *theos* to return in force after postmodernity's calling into question of modernity's powerful *logos*.'[34] They point to the recovery of God-talk beyond the collapse of efforts to save it through links with science and then with anthropology, which we have been tracing in this chapter. For such attempts have clearly not been successful. The modern attempt to save God by making God an appendage of the modern self, from Kant's transcendental ego ensuring the human ethical project to Hegel's divine self underpinning all reality to Levi-Strauss' more scientific self discerned by reflection on cultural and linguistic structures, but already by then no longer in need of God – all of it has faltered. This we see in the gruesome parody of this self met in Schopenhauer, and in Freud subsequently, along with the assertion of historical individuals against this metaphysical self and its God in Feuerbach and Marx, in Nietzsche and the existentialists, then subsequently in Foucault and Derrida. While the self of the modern period was in confident mood, this association of God with the self might have worked, but its critics came rightly or wrongly to insist 'that human life was not enhanced but infantilised by God; that God was not part of human appropriation but human projection; that human beings could only be free when religious belief had been superseded'.[35]

It has been the burden of this chapter to show that modern atheism has its roots in a failed theological strategy. That strategy sought to justify God by making God a part of some allegedly obvious scheme or world-view, be it metaphysical, cosmological or anthropological. But as the scientific world picture eventually excluded the God who had been made dependent on it, so the God linked to the human self in modernity has not survived the liberation of humanity from that self, which has taken place increasingly since the late nineteenth century. As Michael Buckley puts it, 'Argue god as the presupposition or as the corollary of nature; eventually natural philosophy would dispose of god. Argue god as the presupposition or as the corollary of human nature; eventually the denial of god would become an absolute necessity for human existence.'[36] But what if God might indeed be able to stand 'on his own two feet' beyond such associations; indeed, what if God as a theory and a theoretical condition is the god which is dead; what if discredited classical theism is the proper subject of atheism and there is a more real God? The next chapter will take up this issue, looking at contemporary options for the reclaiming of God, as well as pointing to the strong but often forgotten pre-modern roots of such a vision.

Notes

1 John A. T. Robinson, *Honest to God* (London: SCM, 1963).

2 John Shelby Spong, *Why Christianity Must Change or Die? A Bishop Speaks to Believers in Exile* (San Francisco: HarperSanFrancisco, 1998), pp. 49ff.

3 H. P. Owen, *Concepts of Deity* (London: Macmillan, 1971), p. 1.

4 *Ibid.*, pp. 1–2.

5 *Ibid.*, p. 47.

6 Frans Josef van Beeck SJ, *God Encountered: A Contemporary Catholic Systematic Theology*, Vol. 2, Pt 2 (Collegeville, MN: Michael Glazier, 1994), pp. 160–3.

7 Owen, *Concepts*, p. 48.

8 John Macquarrie, *In Search of Deity: An Essay in Dialectical Theism* (London: SCM, 1984), pp. 35–41.

9 *Ibid.*, pp. 39–40.

10 For this insight I thank Dr Peter Carnley, Archbishop of Perth, who pointed this out from his reading of an earlier draft of this chapter.

11 Colin Gunton, *The One, the Three and the Many: God, Creation and the Culture of Modernity* (Cambridge: Cambridge University Press, 1993), pp. 25–6. On the complexity of this issue, Gunton recommends David Nicholls, *Deity and Domination: Images of God and the State in the Nineteenth and Twentieth Centuries* (London: Routledge, 1989).

12 See any standard treatment of modern atheism, e.g. Hans Küng, *Does God Exist?* (1978) (London: Collins, 1980), Pt C.

13 Elizabeth A. Johnson CSJ, *She Who Is: The Mystery of God in Feminist Theological Discourse* (New York: Crossroad, 1993), p. 231.

14 *Ibid.*, p. 225.

15 William C. Placher, *The Domestication of Transcendence: How Modern Thinking about God Went Wrong* (Minneapolis, MN: Westminster John Knox, 1996), p. 76.

16 *Ibid.*, pp. 76–9.

17 Michael J. Buckley SJ, *At the Origins of Modern Atheism* (New Haven: Yale University Press, 1987), p. 343; this is the standard work, offering detailed chapters on Lessius and Mersenne, as well as the other figures mentioned here.

18 *Ibid.*, p. 346.

19 *Ibid.*, pp. 345–6.

20 *Ibid.*, p. 347.

21 *Ibid.*, p. 355.

22 *Ibid.*, p. 222.

23 *Ibid.*

24 *Ibid.*, pp. 223–4.

25 James Byrne, *Glory, Jest and Riddle: Religious Thought in the Enlightenment* (London: SCM, 1996), pp. 163–6.

26 Gunton, *The One*, pp. 28–9.

27 Placher, *Domestication*, p. 92.

28 Wilfred Cantwell Smith, *The Meaning and End of Religion* (1962) (rev. edn, Minneapolis, MN: Fortress, 1991), Ch. 2.

29 Walter Kasper, *The God of Jesus Christ* (1982) (London: SCM, 1984), pp. 9–10.

30 For clarifying my thoughts on the writers considered below, I am indebted to Robert C. Solomon, *Continental Philosophy Since 1750: The Rise and Fall of the Self* (Oxford: Oxford University Press, 1988). Solomon's select bibliography, pp. 206–10, is sufficient to guide the reader to the important primary texts.

31 *Ibid.*, pp. 114–15, 121–2.

32 *Ibid.*, pp. 143–5.

33 *Ibid.*, p. 193.

34 See, e.g. Graham Ward, 'Introduction, or, a guide to theological thinking in cyberspace', in Graham Ward (ed.), *The Postmodern God: A Theological Reader* (Oxford: Blackwell, 1997), pp. xv–xlvii; David Tracy, 'The return of God in contemporary theology', in *On Naming the Present: God, Hermeneutics, and Church* (Concilium Series; Maryknoll, NY: Orbis, 1994), pp. 36–46, p. 42.

35 Buckley, *Origins*, p. 332.

36 *Ibid.*, pp. 332–3.

3 Rethinking God

Modern relational God-talk – Hegelian, process, Trinitarian, modern feminist – solidified as the one permanent achievement of modern theologies of God.

David Tracy, 'The return of God in contemporary theology', 1994

It is not transcendence that is the enemy, but forms of the one that fail to give due space to the many.

Colin Gunton, *The One, the Three and the Many*, 1993

Old gods are no good;
they are smaller than they promise, or else they are large
like mountains, leaning over
the soul to admire themselves.

R. S. Thomas, 'Hesitations'

We have seen how belief in God has become problematic, and increasingly irreconcilable with mainstream Western life. And we have noted the complicity of theology in these facts of its own estrangement; the God co-opted since the seventeenth century for cosmological and anthropological duty has subsequently been made redundant. Now we ask if all this is inevitable. In this chapter we inquire whether alternative understandings of God can carry us beyond the fatally linked options of theism and atheism, past both theistic acceptance and atheistic rejection of the remote God – all-powerful, all-knowing, all-sufficient in 'himself'.

In the first part of this chapter, aspects of the more relational God-talk typical of current theology will be considered. Known variously as 'dialectical theism', 'dipolar theism', 'neoclassical theism' or 'panentheism', this is an attempt to hold together the transcendence of God, which was the burden of classical theism, with the immanence of God. This immanence has resonances in mystical and romantic sensibility, in the Christian narratives of Christ's incarnation and passion, in the Old and New Testament conceptions of Spirit, and nowadays in the thoroughly relational cosmology, ecology and anthropology which are everywhere on the rise.

As well as concepts, however, in the second part of this chapter we will consider images, for a number of organic attempts are currently underway to reimagine God beyond 'Monarch', 'Father' and other images that have for many people reinforced God's remoteness.

In the third part of this chapter, we recall the burden of our previous chapter, to show that God was not always imagined as fatally disconnected from the world and from human life. In the previous chapter the transformation of God-talk from the seventeenth century was rehearsed; here we look past Hegel, Whitehead and other modern exponents of a more holistic theism to a tradition of long Christian provenance; apart from this chapter's panentheistic slice through the history of Christian thought, we can also point to a fuller sense of God in relation to life in mainstream Christian tradition, though always matching this immanent theme with a strong sense of God's unknowability.

In the fourth part of this chapter, attention shifts to Trinitarian images of God. Modern relational God-talk shares the burden of traditional Trinitarian formulations, balancing the otherness and hiddenness of God with the immediacy of God met in Christ and in the spiritual life. Indeed, it may well be that Trinitarian considerations are at work in the formulation of today's holistic concepts and images of God. So rather than a novelty, holistic concepts and images of God are seen to be at the heart of Christian God-talk comprehensively conceived.

Beyond classical theism: ideas

John Macquarrie has long argued that religion has two poles, and that varieties of religions range between the immanent deities of polytheism, pantheism and animism leading to fetishism, on the one hand, and the high Gods of monotheism (Judaism, Islam) leading in the direction of complete separation of God from the world (dualism) and eventually to atheism, on the other. Christianity rightly understood holds the two poles together in what he calls 'existential–ontological theism'[1] and, later, 'dialectical theism'. The assessment Macquarrie makes, in keeping with the argument of my last chapter, is that atheism flourishes where finite and infinite are in competition. This point, to which we will return in conversation with Colin Gunton in his discussion of the Trinity later in this chapter, is made by Macquarrie in his Gifford Lectures for 1983–84.[2] There he seeks to hold together a view of God as genuinely transcendent, rather than God as merely a dimension of reality alongside the material universe, while at the same time resisting downplaying of the world in favour of God, which as we have seen leads straight to atheism. This is closer to theism than to pantheism, Macquarrie asserts, though he wishes with John Robinson to retain a key insight from pantheism: that God is the inner reality of everything (though for Robinson what we cannot tolerate of pantheism is its characteristic impassive, impersonal view of life and its playing-down of evil,[3] which is not such an issue with theism).

Tensions in God-talk

Macquarrie sets out the nature of this more relational, holistic theism with a series of illuminating tensions.[4]

The first is between being and nothing. God is the 'ground of being', but is not simply equated with being, in a way that we have seen to be typical of a major Western tradition (though a tradition radically challenged in recent postmodern thought). Instead of this too-simple identification, Macquarrie joins Tillich and others in declaring God to be beyond existence and non-existence, and in this sense strictly nothing, *no-thing*. Here he favours the expression of John Scotus Eriugena (of whom more shortly) that God is 'He who is more than being'.

Second is the tension between the one and the many. This is an attempt to say that God holds all things together but is not some undifferentiated glue, as in pantheism. Rather, God holds all the richness of being in Godself, while at the same time expressing that being in the created world. This distinction between 'primordial' and 'expressive being', as Macquarrie puts it, is similar to the distinction between the primordial and the consequent natures of God that we meet in Whitehead and the process theologians, who emphasize an unchanging and transcendent pole in God as well as a more malleable pole immanent in and influenced by the world.

Third, there is the juxtaposition between knowability and incomprehensibility, which allows a different take on the same idea. The God Macquarrie struggles to name is both the unknown mysterious depth of existence, and also the meaning of everything, grasped as a vision of the worth and meaning of the whole.

A fourth point makes clear that transcendence and immanence are not two parts of God, nor that God in one mode of being or one type of action is immanent while in another mode God is transcendent. Here we discern a difference between Macquarrie's dialectical theism and the very significant dipolarity which process theology imagines in its God. The point here is that God needs to be imagined as both wholly immanent and wholly transcendent. This was the burden of early Trinitarian formulation up to the Council of Nicaea, and it hints at Trinitarian themes lying in the background of modern relational God-talk (a point to which we will return later in this chapter).

Macquarrie's fifth tension is that between impassability and passability. Here reason contributes the conviction that love cannot be had without vulnerability, while Scripture regularly offers us a passionate God of intense feeling. But Macquarrie wishes to avoid the excesses of those commentators ancient and modern who ascribe suffering to God in ways that undermine God's power actually to deal with the causes of suffering, leaving us with nothing more than what Don Cupitt once called a 'puny godling'. 'Without his [God's] passability, his sharing in our affliction, there would be no bond of sympathy between him and us,' Macquarrie writes; 'Without his impass-ability, his power to absorb and transform, there could be no final faith in God.'[5]

The sixth and final tension is between eternity and temporality in God. On the one hand, timelessness is readily explicable in terms of God transcending successiveness and the forces of entropy, while proving constant and faith-ful. But with this faithfulness must come solidarity, patience with human slowness and, in general, a willingness on God's part to work with humans at their own pace, as with the cosmos over long periods of evolution. This insight is nicely captured by Japanese theologian Kosuke Koyama in his claim that God's speed is three miles per hour – this is the speed God walks because it is the speed humans walk, and so it must be if the timeless God is to walk alongside us.[6]

Interestingly, Macquarrie is unsure about the ultimate provenance of his favoured view of God. He believes that it is really a philosophical theism, and is concerned that it may not suit the God of the Bible. Macquarrie is certainly an advocate of natural theology, arguing that knowledge of God emerges from natural human reason which postulates a transcendent abso-lute. Though he has recognized that the same reason also demands greater involvement from that absolute, if it is to have any credibility and emotional appeal. One could say that this is also a very scriptural faith, however, indebted both to the covenanting, confronting, punishing and forgiving God of the Hebrew Scriptures and the incarnate, dying and raised figure of God-with-us from the New Testament.

As mentioned, Macquarrie the philosophical theologian is concerned that his God is too much the fruit of philosophy, and as we shall see in the second part of this chapter its history is traced back to a fourth-century philosopher, Plotinus, and has triumphed in the twentieth century thanks to another philosopher, Whitehead (though a number of card-carrying Christians also pass the torch of this alternative tradition along, as we will note). But what strikes me is the heavily imagistic tone of this enterprise, which even Macquarrie admits when he asserts that the religious and the imagistic is as important in this undertaking as the philosophic and the conceptual.[7] Perhaps this is another tension that ought to be included in our appropria-tion of dialectical theism, between affective and cognitive, both of which have a place in the provenance of belief – this recognition gives us a good reason to consider recently sprung images of God that help give imaginative flesh to the concepts we have been considering. For it is this imaginative failure of God-images to engage the interest, the imagination, the passion and commitment, the 'spirituality' of secular people that has led to social entrenchment of the atheism that emerged from earlier failures of imagina-tion, as we saw in the previous chapter. And atheism is not the only result of such failure, but also the boredom and disconnection from faith and its symbols which burden many who stay with the Church. So with a view to how we might redress this lack, identified in our first chapter above, we now turn to images of God that express both reassuring transcendence and engaging immanence.

Beyond classical theism: images

It is important to realize what old, established, monarchical images of God and new, holistic images of God have in common. And that is that both are sets of *images*; neither is the real thing. Sallie McFague is correct to point out that 'Father' as an image of God is neither more nor less literal than 'Mother' as an image of God, although the former is far more entrenched in tradition and more familiar than the latter, having become petrified into a definition.[8]

Embodied in the world

With this warning in mind, the first image we will consider is of God as soul of the universe, and the universe as God's body. Often this image uses 'world' rather than 'universe' – no doubt 'world' conjures up images of familiar, beautiful planet Earth rather than unfamiliar, cold, remote outer space, and hence makes for a more engaging religious symbol (though it does seem to me 'terracentric' to emphasize the Earth at the expense of the universe, and to compromise the holism and interconnectedness such an image aims to foster). This conception of the world as God's body has many resonances in mysticism and romantic sensibility, and in theology, from Gerard Manley Hopkins to Teilhard de Chardin – it is an image admirably suited to the dipolar theism of process theology.[9] The history of this image is traced by one of its major proponents, Grace Jantzen.[10] Among other things it is a model favoured by Jantzen because it offers a more positive catholic attitude to the world of matter than the Platonic tradition which has prospered in Christianity. It also strikes her as more realistic about human personhood, in that God imagined as a 'person' is appreciated more holistically by recalling that to be a person is to have a body. And here she insists that disembodied persons are just too problematic philosophically.[11]

Another reason for the attractiveness of the image is the purchase it gives on the problem of God's action in the world. To investigate this thorny issue will be our burden in the next chapters, but for now we note that a God embodied in the world can be imagined to know the state of the world with the sort of immediate awareness by which we know the states of our own bodies, and that divine influence is not by external intervention but can be imagined analogously to how we influence parts of our own bodies. Jantzen bluntly asserts that it is no sillier to say that God *feels* sensations than to say that God *knows* data about things, in that both are images.[12] It is just that Western body–soul dualism in its Platonic and Cartesian forms is more comfortable with knowledge and minds than with sensations and bodies when it imagines God.

For McFague the embodied God is a good metaphor because it remythologizes the suffering love that we discern in the cross of Christ, casting it in terms of God's radical personal commitment to the cosmos. Also it allows the vulnerability of God to be imaged, without putting God at risk of being destroyed by the 'big crunch', or any other cosmic denouement.[13] But how is God to escape this fate, if the identification of God and world is so strong as to attract the charges of pantheism that McFague and Jantzen have attracted (despite their efforts to distinguish what they are doing from pantheism)? The answer is in the insistence that we are more than our bodies.[14] As Jantzen puts it, 'If human embodiment does not reduce personal significance to physiology, neither would the postulate that God's body is the universe mean that God is finally describable in purely physical terms.'[15]

This whole idea is dismissed out of hand by John Polkinghorne largely on the grounds that our universe is just too unlike a body. As bodies decay into senility and death, so the universe as God's body fails to resemble a real body. And as the universe may well have emerged from a fluctuating vacuum field, does that mean that God was once a rich but nevertheless minimal vacuum, and that after the 'big crunch', God will become something else? Polkinghorne also claims that if the universe is God's body, then it must be organic. And despite the 'Gaia' hypothesis of James Lovelock, claiming just this of the Earth, that it is an organism, Polkinghorne is unconvinced 'because of that lack of appropriate degree of reflexive complexity within Earth's admittedly many and delicately balanced relationships'.[16]

Polkinghorne's points are well made, and Jantzen does take her image rather literally. Like any analogy it is limited, and does not bear overmuch attention. But the fruitfulness of the image is as important as its accuracy. We do not consider it necessary to critique the Trinity because three persons cannot at the same time be one person. We recognize this to be paradoxical talk, and that this is what is intended by it. We do not need to say that God as King is a poor image because we cannot see God's crown, or God's castle. We do not need to say that God as Father is a poor image because we cannot point to God's pipe and slippers! While there may be other reasons to query these images, for instance because of their use as hardened definitions to direct the Church in particular ways, they are not queried for their inappropriateness when pressed too far. I am sure that Polkinghorne would consent to God being imaged in personal terms, without being put off by the fact that persons have bodies and eventually die. Nor do I think we need be overliteral in our use of other, less familiar images, such as the world as God's body.

For our purposes God embodied in the world is a powerful image because it is powerfully sacramental, reinforcing a catholic sense of the sacredness of matter and of life in the world that many Roman Catholics as well as Orthodox, Anglicans and Protestants no longer sense in their churches. To be in constant touch with God, as this image suggests, presses wonderfully on the modern imagination, and really does affirm with Hopkins that 'The world is charged with the grandeur of God', which will indeed (if thus we see things) 'flame out, like shining from shook foil'.[17] The image is a powerful one for its shock value, its disorienting and reorienting potential,[18] as is the case for others we will soon consider. This is important for an imaginative reminting of theism, given the distaste of atheists, and the waning interest of many believers.

The image of the world as God's body fosters ecological responsibility, too, on the part of that element of God's body which is conscious and shares God's image – the human race. The demythologized world of modernity (that has brought us so much good by clearing a way for science through superstition) must now be befriended, and remythologized. For the enemy now is no longer a superstition which stifles the liberating power of technology, but rather that technology itself, which when bereft of a love and respect for the world becomes in turn an even more dangerous superstition, one of empty and dangerous instrumentalism and utilitarianism. We note, in conclusion, that this is an image of God which will not denigrate the natural or the human at the expense of the spiritual. And for this reason it is not an image as prone to atheistic takeover as we have seen theistic images to be, which tend to dualism and remoteness.

The image we have been considering is not a personal image of God, because persons are more than their bodies. McFague proceeds to commend more explicitly personal images, however, because we know them from the inside, and hence they are maximally imaginatively engaging – they are the richest images available, given our human inability to imagine a fuller category of being than the personal, and because they are images that can tend in the directions of relationality, interdependence and other holistic virtues that are desperately needed today for securing the future of life on Earth.[19]

God as mother of the world

The first personal image we consider is the image of God as mother. This is an image that emphasizes creation and not just redemption – the birthing, nurturing, healing mother is concerned with establishing life and through intimate involvement bringing life to fulfilment, while Father images have too often been employed in ways which have underplayed any sense of nurture in favour of discipline themes, of schooling in righteousness, and of judgement. The fourteenth-century mystic Julian of Norwich is most famous for use of maternal images of God in the Western tradition. Yet it is very contemporary imagery in terms of the ethic of care for the world it underwrites, which is necessary in the light of our increasingly urgent ecological dilemma.[20]

This image receives a most creative twist at the hands of Arthur Peacocke, the English priest–scientist and theologian, in his 1978 Bampton Lectures. Rather than mother as someone who brings us to birth but also nurtures us to mature adulthood, this is an image of mother and foetus, with the world imagined as created and nurtured within the being of God.[21] One of McFague's students, Anna Case-Winters, takes it up. She believes that to say the world is God's body as Jantzen does is to overidentify God with the world. But as a pregnant woman is clearly more than the womb and its contents, so God in this image is more than the world while nevertheless fully integrated with the world, nurturing it and depended upon by it. Case-Winters imagines a 'transcendence that is not distant or over and above but rather embracing and surrounding in an immanent fashion'.[22] She insists on the *world* as the foetus, rather than the human individual, to get away from connotations of individual overdependence on the mother,[23] while Jantzen points out the opposite risk: that the foetus will grow separate from the mother to the point of birth and complete distinction, which tends to dualism and undermines the organic aim of the image.[24]

Perhaps McFague is on stronger ground by promoting the mother image without emphasizing the corresponding foetus image for the world, which allows the integral link between mother and child begun in gestation and continued in nurture through the life cycle to be highlighted without infantilizing or else alienating the recipient of the nurture. But however this card is played, it does suggest strong dipolarity, and offers an imaginative, holistic and ethically fruitful way of thinking about the relation of God with the world. And when placed alongside the image of the world as God's body, it makes the problem of divine action easier, a problem which becomes most intractable when God is declared to be wholly outside the world. But more of this in the subsequent chapters.

God as lover

Another suggestive image is that of God as lover. This is strongly favoured by the process theologian Norman Pittenger. His talk of God as 'Love-in-Act', and of we ourselves as 'lovers in the making' through our life of exposure to the love of God, is in keeping with the notion of God's love as a 'lure' in Pittenger's theology.[25] It is God's aim to extract the best potential of every event, and certainly with human lives. It is an image picturing God very positively as the champion of human thriving, which is a corrective to the opposite claim of humanistic atheism.

But Sallie McFague goes further to highlight the sexual dimension of this image of God as lover, insisting that love without a component of desire is bloodless, cold and sterile. Eros, with its celebration of passionate attraction and desire for unity, is not a mainstream God-image to be sure. But from the Song of Songs in the Hebrew Scriptures to imagery of brides and bridegrooms in New Testament epistle, Gospel and apocalyptic, it is an image ripe for the plucking. And as McFague points out, it has been a theme of the tradition from Augustine to Aquinas to the Westminster Confession that the spiritual goal of Christians is to 'know' God and 'enjoy' God forever.[26]

A good thing about this image is that lovers seek a response, and there is nothing detached about it, as there is for instance about the image of a monarch, or of a mother – indeed, even of a friend, which is the image we consider next. McFague is also enthusiastic about the way this image portrays divine love for human beings as 'because of' rather than 'in spite of', which is how divine love is often portrayed – that God loves us in spite of our sins, in spite of who we really are.[27] In a romantic culture like that of the contemporary West, when sexuality is often the most sacred element of secular life, the image of God as lover is full of imaginative resonance. It is a dipolar image up to a point – the unity of lover and beloved is something to be achieved, rather than something already abiding as the state of things, working best when there is a conscious love in return. But of course this is not always forthcoming from human beings. So we might find the image of God as unrequited lover of the world suggestive, as did the writer of Hosea, Chapters 1 and 2, who used this image to illustrate God's covenant faithfulness to an unfaithful people. This is a God who, in words from the Johannine prologue, 'came to his own people, and his own people received him not'. Still, without the human response of love this image will not render best service as the organic image we seek – an image which without reducing God to the world nevertheless establishes a profound link.

God as friend, as mentor

The next personal image to be mentioned is that of God as friend. McFague makes the point that friends are as or more important than mothers and lovers, bonding with us in relationships of free choice with an emphasis on mutuality, equality and reciprocity. It is true of friends that they simply like each other, and are bound together in ways which are less exclusive and turned-inward than lovers. There are dipolar elements here, although God's dealing with the world according to this model is optional while more organic models suggest a constitutive bond.[28]

Frans Josef van Beeck offers a variant of this image when he conceives of God along the lines of a mentor. In a discussion of revelation, van Beeck points out how a good mentor is transcendent from the relationship, not needing the relationship for the mentor's own edification, who remains in the best sense 'disinterested'. 'Only an unconditional, all-enabling Presence is transcendent enough to move our innermost immanence to open itself to others without anxiety about ourselves,' van Beeck writes.[29] Such an image maintains the traditional theme of divine impassability in a creative way while nevertheless capturing the sense in which a mentor thoroughly shapes and, more importantly, becomes part of the one who is the object of their care. And here the idea of God immanent within the world completes the dipolarity of this image, with God immanent in the ones being creatively influenced. What is good about this is that humanity is befriended by God, not disliked or disapproved of. It is indeed an image to foster an adult relationship between Christians and God, which is one of ease and mutuality rather than cowering submission. And anything adult on the part of Christianity is a challenge to the atheistic claim that the faith infantilizes its adherents.

The Force be with you

There is one other image which is personal but not derived from the realm of human intimacy that I will mention. And that image comes not from a theologian but from a film-maker. George Lucas, whose epic *Star Wars* saga is at the time of writing spawning a sequence of 'prequels', gives us a subtle and nuanced image of God as 'the Force'. BBC religion producer Peter Armstrong strongly favours this as an engaging image of God, whereas he found the Tillichian ground of being offered by Bishop Robinson in *Honest to God* to be a philosophical stone instead of religious bread.[30] 'The Force' is an unseen spiritual reality which nevertheless guides, illuminates and protects the righteous in their battle with evil. It is accessible to spiritual adepts and warrior knights, so this space opera goes, to the extent of their discipline and single-mindedness. There is also a tendency away from dualism toward the notion of a 'dark side of the force', which is evil and chaotic, and which too has its adepts. 'The Force' is certainly intimately related to the world and its progress toward the good, but it is clearly transcendent and mysterious also.

This is an image compatible with God's Spirit seen as a power in the world, coming to expression in individuals, though falling short of the Spirit as it is defined with reference to Jesus and his ongoing project throughout the New Testament. And 'the Force' certainly falls short of the personal nature of God's Spirit as that notion develops through the Biblical tradition. In *Star Wars* the young hero is encouraged to use 'the Force' like a technology, which recalls pre-theistic notions of sacred power such as mana. There are hints of the personal about it, but not sufficiently so for it to function as an image of the living God. But it may take us some way toward imaginatively conceiving how God as soul of the world might operate in that world. In other words, a more (though not as we have seen an entirely) personal image could annexe this image of the 'Force' and use it to explicate the nature of its connection with the world.

In this section, I have examined a range of God-images which give imaginative flesh to the conceptual bones of panentheism, dipolar theism or else 'dialectical theism'.[31] They have a newness and freshness which is energizing and arresting. This is what we want from a God-image – liveliness, interest, engagement. Perhaps the image of the world as God's body allows a more cosmic, ecological focus without completely sacrificing the personal. Because we know the intimate experience of embodiedness, we can connect imaginatively or by analogy to the image in a way which is significantly personal, without it being an image of human relationship. No longer ought we to favour exclusively certain images such as monarchical ones, when we know they are compromised through their remoteness from a holistic world-view and their support of extreme social and religious conservatism. It is important to remember that the more familiar images remain images, and nothing more than images, despite their familiarity. In the next section of the chapter, we will consider just how new this more holistic theism is.

An alternative tradition

John Macquarrie charts a history for the dialectical theism he favours. It begins with philosophy and ends with philosophy. Plotinus introduces it in his Neoplatonic philosophy, while its most distinctive modern champions are G. W. F. Hegel, Martin Heidegger and Alfred North Whitehead. Hence Macquarrie's sense that this is first and foremost a philosophical theism that may not serve specifically Christian purposes. Our discussion of images of God has reassured us, however, that specifically Christian themes about the concrete commitment of God to history which is Jesus Christ, and the call to ethical responsibility, are the motivation for many who advance it. Plotinus was certainly pre-Christian, and while Hegel thought himself a Christian (indeed, a Lutheran) neither he nor Whitehead is deemed to be orthodox, no doubt for want of attention to the full scope of Christian faith in their work. And despite the significant attention of theologians such as Tillich, Bultmann, Gogarten, Rahner, Macquarrie and Cupitt to the work of Heidegger, this lapsed Roman Catholic is not normally reckoned as 'orthodox'. But between these figures of philosophy ancient and modern there are a range of quite specifically and self-consciously Christian philosophical witnesses.[32]

Key figures in 'dipolar theism'

Plotinus is the favoured starting point because of his dipolar understanding of 'The One' who emanates into creation down a divine hierarchy of mind then of soul. This is not the Christian doctrine of the Trinity nor that of creation, but it does influence the first Christian Macquarrie mentions, who is Pseudo-Dionysius. Sometimes this fourth-century figure is seen as a pantheist, and at other times is seen as thoroughly committed to the transcendence of God. The dipolarity of his theism is reflected in the fact that both assessments are true. His God is above intellection, being, even above deity, and yet is transported outwards into creation in an ecstasy of divine love to participate in the orders of being in creation (though mostly in the higher ones).[33]

This line of influence continues in an 'Irish-born Scot' called John, John Scotus Eriugena, who translated Pseudo-Dionysius. Here one finds God as a dimension of reality, not a part of nature but not separable either from any part of creation. While the God of Eriugena is the creator who is not created, nevertheless God is also self-creating through these works. One cannot help thinking of Whitehead's 'consequent nature' of God here, which changes in response to creation, while the primordial nature does not. This is more the case with Nicholas of Cusa (1401–1464) who emphasizes that God is both 'absolute maximum' and 'restricted maximum', rather than a God beyond any distinction, as with Eriugena. In *De docta ignorantia*, Cusa commends a 'learned ignorance' upon which Macquarrie draws when insisting that God is at once transcendent and immanent, maintaining the paradox. His pan-entheism is presented in the *Apology*, where God is in the world in the same way that a cause is 'in' that which is caused, but God is not to be identified with creation; 'the universe is in God and stands in intimate relation to him,' Cusa writes, 'but it does not exhaust his being.'[34]

In Gottfried Wilhelm Leibniz (1646–1716) we have an extraordinary early-modern synthesis which has profoundly influenced Whitehead more recently. Beyond the particulate, atomistic universe of seventeenth-century materialistic science on the one hand, and the monism of Spinoza on the other hand, Leibniz offered a view of reality in terms of three levels of 'monads', with God as the highest and most special monad. The monads have rudiments of mind, and together with God form a unified, organic whole.[35]

In Alfred North Whitehead (1861–1947) we have a modern advocate for dipolar theism. His indebtedness to this tradition, most immediately to Leibniz, is clear. Whitehead's metaphysics sees a world made up of actual entities called events, and because he is a 'panpsychist' like Leibniz, finding a mental pole in all entities, he believes that every event 'prehends' (unconsciously apprehends) every other event. Like the special monad of Leibniz, Whitehead's God is the most special of the actual entities and the only eternal one, hence prehending every other entity – influencing them, but also being influenced (thus the world also creates God). This God has a complete, transcendent 'primordial nature' and an incomplete 'consequent nature', through which God interacts with the world. Macquarrie is clear that God so conceived is rather too coordinate with the rest of reality to be a fully Christian God.[36] Nevertheless Whitehead's metaphysics spawned the extensive and varied school of process theology, and has proved enormously suggestive for those who appreciate the fully relational cosmology of modern physics.

Departures from classical theism in mainstream tradition

But for all this it is important to note that divine remoteness from the world and from human life, which has characterized classical theism, is foreign to a great deal of pre-modern faith in its mainstream expressions. It is not just a matter of a minority panentheistic tradition being unearthed to underwrite the reconception of God in dialectical terms, as we see in Macquarrie, but rediscovering a more widespread balance between transcendence and immanence. William Placher seeks to demonstrate this with reference to three classic figures of pre-modern theology: Aquinas, Luther and Calvin.

Aquinas is regularly portrayed as the champion of a philosophical and speculative account of God. We saw how this assessment emerged in the last chapter, when Cajetan and Suarez were identified as precursors of prominent later readings of Aquinas as a rationalist. But Placher makes much of passages in the *Summa theologiae* which emphasize the mystery and unknowability of God. 'Now we cannot know what God is, but only what he is not', writes Aquinas; 'we must therefore consider the ways in which God does not exist rather than the ways in which he does.'[37] This early statement in the *Summa* strikes Placher as definitive and programmatic. In light of it he approaches the famous 'five ways' or proofs of God's existence which are perhaps Aquinas' best known legacy. But where at the end of each argument, from first cause through to design, does Aquinas say 'and this proves the existence of God'? For Placher, the simple repeated comments 'to which everyone gives the name "God" ' or 'and this we call "God" ' at the end of the proofs simply indicates that Aquinas was pointing to the orientation of the human mind toward God in all its perceiving, but not at all the reachability of God by the human mind out of human reason alone. Even concerning the doctrine of analogy, by which he is thought to offer some access to God's nature by analogy with our own nature, Aquinas admits that such words 'simply mean certain perfections without any indications of how these perfections are possessed'.[38] God for Aquinas is not the graspable end of a metaphysical system able to make complete sense of the world, according to Placher – Aquinas is offering metalinguistic rules, not metaphysical systems.[39] And while it may sound as though this God is indeed very remote from human experience and life in the world, nevertheless what is beyond reach of the reason is not remote from faith, which is 'an act of mind assenting to the divine truth by virtue of the command of the will as this is moved by God through grace'.[40] Part 3 of the *Summa* is where Placher believes we must look to find the nearness, the Christianness, of Aquinas' God, as he discusses Christ and the sacraments, with participation in the life of grace and the experience of the Spirit deemed essential for knowing God.[41]

Placher also discusses Luther and Calvin, who in their distinct but complementary ways witness to a God made known through close involvement in the world and in human struggle, but not by speculation which retreats from distinctively Christian sources. No one is more non-speculative than Luther, who damns the 'godless temerity that, where God has humiliated Himself in order to become recognisable, man seeks for himself another way'.[42] Luther's hidden God is discerned by faith in the cross and in the travail of the world, not remote but actively involved. But this is the Spirit's work to help us discern, for Luther, rather than the work of reason. So too with Calvin, for whom reason and human capacities cannot mount up to knowledge of God – only God's involvement in the world for us provides access: 'It is not necessary for us to mount up on high to inquire about what must be hidden from us at this moment. For God lowers himself to us. He knows us only in his Son – as though he says, "Here I am. Contemplate me." '[43] And while Calvin held against Luther that there was more to God than was made known in Christ (the 'extra Calvinisticum'), nevertheless this need not be read as anything more than divine accommodation to human limitations – it does not mean that there is a difference between God as revealed and God somehow remote in Godself.

In these three witnesses of pre-modern theology we discern a different message from that of classical theism and those who think that it provides the Christian norm. The thrust of what we have met here, we would have to say, is *faith rather than speculation*. Nor do we discern harmful ideological baggage in this gracious God of revelation and salvation, this Trinitarian God, this deconstructed King of Kings and Lord of Lords whose apparent predisposition is to draw near to the world and embrace the human race. There is neither 'speculative' nor 'ideological captivity' here. In the next chapter, the double agency doctrine of divine action will be presented – another pre-modern tradition of close divine involvement in the world.

The Trinity

We must not forget that the God of Jesus Christ is Trinitarian. And it is a cause of some embarrassment to recent theology that God has been talked about so much since the Enlightenment without reference to the Trinity. But that oversight is being corrected in theology today.

Trinitarian talk arose from convictions about the uniqueness of Jesus and the Church's sense of Jesus' continuing presence in the power of his Gospel during the New Testament period, issuing in the full-blown orthodoxy of one God subsisting in three modes of reality by the fourth century – the Trinity is the vivid experience of revelation and salvation rendered into doctrine. Even H. P. Owen knows that it is a long way from these wellsprings of distinctively Christian God-talk to the definition of classical theism offered early in Chapter 2. The lean charms of the latter were to prove far more 'reasonable', however, and far more popular.

The eclipse of the Trinity

The damage was done by the Cappadocian Fathers around the time of the Nicene Creed, according to Catherine Mowry LaCugna in an influential study. Despite their best efforts to arrive at a 'metaphysics of the economy of salvation', they nevertheless separated an inner divine essence in God (the 'immanent Trinity') from what could be known about God through God's self-manifestation in creation and salvation (the 'economic Trinity'). This separation widened as the Eastern Church employed mediating divine energies to bridge the gap between God and the world, according to the authoritative fourteenth-century Byzantine theologian Gregory Palamas.

The Western story is equally parlous, according to LaCugna, beginning with Augustine's novel psychological analogies of the Trinity and his shift to talk about a divine essence behind the three persons, which gave rise to a Western focus on the interior life of God at the expense of God being encountered fully in God's acts. This emphasis on the immanent over the economic Trinity led in Aquinas to treatises where *De deo uno* was separated from *De deo trino*. According to LaCugna this sold out the Trinity to the bare monotheism of classical theism thereafter.[44] As Karl Rahner, who has led the way in reclaiming a Trinitarian understanding of God in recent theology, wryly remarked, 'we must be willing to admit that, should the doctrine of the Trinity have to be dropped as false, the major part of religious literature will remain virtually unchanged.'[45]

William C. Placher argues that despite early impulses away from Trinitarian toward speculative God-talk, any such trend was not powerfully manifest in the West until the seventeenth century. As for Christian tradition in the pre-modern period to which LaCugna refers, Placher points to significant Trinitarian emphases in Aquinas when revelation and salvation are discussed, to the Trinitarian shape of Luther's anti-speculative theology and to Calvin, for whom unless God is thought of as Triune, 'only the bare and empty name of God flits about in our brains, to the exclusion of the true God'.[46] But from the seventeenth century Placher can point to the eagerness of deists to be free of 'the incomprehensible jargon of the Trinitarian arithmetic' (Thomas Jefferson), and of Socinians (who evolved into Unitarians in America) to defeat it by recourse to their rationalistic reading of the Bible[47] – trends which came to characterize both scepticism and liberal theology in the eighteenth and nineteenth centuries. This marginalization of the Trinity accompanied the retreat of theology from holistic God-talk to the use of God in aid of a working metaphysics, which led in turn to atheism, as we saw in the last chapter. For Placher it was the hardening of such

speculative impulses in the seventeenth century which finally made Trinitarian thinking seem irrationally founded and otiose, whereas before that in
pre-modernity a far more recognizably Christian theism had prevailed,
despite contradictory impulses he concedes to LaCugna. For today's believers and unbelievers alike, like it or not, it is this philosophically tinged
monotheism rather than the relational, less speculatively driven Trinitarian
vision that is taken to be Christian belief.

The recovery of the Trinity

But in theology today the Trinity is being revived with a vengeance. In the
hands of many writers of various overarching commitments it is seen to take
us beyond what Colin Gunton in his 1992 Bampton Lectures calls 'the
single, arbitrarily willing deity of so much of the Christian and anti-Christian
tradition'.[48]

Following the Western trend toward a single Godhead existing in three
modalities, we have Rahner's treatment as mentioned above, which is
closely attuned to the Trinity disclosed in the economy of salvation. And we
have the offering of John Macquarrie which finds the Trinity in the realm of
natural theology – metaphysics gives us 'Being', and 'Being' has primordial,
expressive and unitive dimensions, which correspond to Father, Son and
Holy Spirit.[49] But for Macquarrie, clearly, God comes first and the Trinity
comes second, as an interpretation, while for Rahner there is no warrant to
separate God in Godself from God as revealed in the economy of salvation.

Following the Eastern emphasis on the threeness of divine persons,
finding their unity not in some Godhead but in the Father, from whom the
Son and the Spirit proceed, we have a corresponding recent emphasis on
Trinitarian sociality. The priority of relationship in a world of division and
opposition is commended with reference to the divine life, which is understood as a relationship of great individual richness and yet constitutive
interdependence. And a life moreover which spills out into the economy of
creation and redemption, with the Spirit closing the circle by returning all
things at last to the Father through the Son. This ancient theme finds a
recent representative in Leonardo Boff,[50] for whom the social alienation of
class and wealth is challenged by a liberating Gospel: that in the beginning of
everything there is communion, not separateness.

But here as frequently elsewhere liberation theology owes much to Jürgen
Moltmann,[51] who champions the Eastern emphasis on divine sociality and
has offered seminal reflections on the Trinity in response to the problem of
evil. Moltmann's Trinity promises the consummation of cosmic history as
the reinfolding of creation into the love of God the Father. This theology of
hope is not the putting-off of answers to present suffering, however. While
Moltmann allows no speculative, theistic answer to evil and suffering, he

does find a 'working answer' in theology of the cross – in theology given to meditation on what the cross of Jesus can tell us about God, rather than speculation about what human reason can tell us about God.

Following Paul and Luther in this enterprise, Moltmann also responds to the despair characteristic of much twentieth-century experience, which he shared as a prisoner of the British at the end of the Second World War. Moltmann accepts the protest atheism of those who cannot reconcile an omnipotent God with human suffering. Perhaps omnipotence can be reinterpreted, however, as the power of suffering love to soften hearts and rekindle hope. Of God, Moltmann insists that 'He is no "cold heavenly power", nor does he "tread his way over corpses", but is known as the human God in the crucified Son of Man.'[52] In this sense, of God caught up in the negativity of the cross, Moltmann accepts that he is a panentheist, whose God is present everywhere, even in the midst of evil, while nevertheless remaining transcendent. This is not speculation, however, as Moltmann insists, but merely reflection on what the cross discloses.[53] From these beginnings Moltmann's project develops into a Trinitarian mysticism of suffering whereby 'The Father is crucifying love, the Son is crucified love and the Holy Spirit is the unvanquishable power of the cross.'[54]

In both the approaches just encountered, of the Western and Eastern varieties – the one God in three modes on the one hand, the divine community of persons on the other – the attempt is made to conceive of transcendence and immanence together, in keeping with the thrust of much contemporary theology. The one God manifest in three modes of being is anything but remote from the world. This is a God profoundly involved in the world through the immanent Word, *Logos* or Son, who is the inner principle of reality become concrete in the particularity of a historical life. And this is a God understood to be at work establishing that inner principle in ever greater manifestations of concreteness through the Holy Spirit, until 'Christ is all in all'. The communitarian God suggests a relational theism in a different way, by revealing relationship and community as the content of divine life. This ontological priority of community, this relational nature of God, is understood to be implanted into things by God in the unfolding of creation. But it also represents the thrust of divine mission in the world, with the Kingdom of God understood to be the presently emerging and finally universal triumph of relationship in a world made for relationship but too often the home of alienation.

Reconciling the one and the many

In this study I am commending a reimagining of God in ways that resonate with our newly sprung relational vision of reality, beyond the remoteness of much theism. The panentheism addressed earlier in this chapter through concepts and images variously achieves this, without God either vanishing over the horizon by too much transcendence or melting into the world through too much immanence. Because in either event the world and humanity are diminished and threatened.

Colin Gunton, in his 1992 Bampton Lectures, discusses this undertaking in terms of classic philosophical tensions between 'the one' and 'the many'.[55] The world we now know is profoundly diverse yet deeply unified. But at the level of human history this balance has been undermined since the onset of modernity. Modernity, according to Gunton, means the rejection of God, 'the one', the absolute, in favour of the freedom of 'the many'. But, paradoxically, seven devils worse than the first moved into the modern world subsequently and made their dwelling there. The role of God as the unifying centre of life was usurped by various modern ideologies, from communist or fascist totalitarianism to late capitalism with its strongly homogenizing consumer culture, all of which in their overmastering zeal have enslaved rather than liberated the many in repressive cultures of conformity. Postmodernity is not fundamentally different from modernity, according to Gunton, who follows the 'late-modern' and 'late capitalist' interpretation of postmodernity characteristic of Fredric Jameson[56] and David Harvey.[57] Except that where modernity ignored 'the other' in one or another stifling ideological monism, postmodernity sidelines the other in a new monism of 'the individual' – the individual ego blows up to become the defining centre of reality, subsuming 'the other' as surely as would any totalizing ideology of modernity.

Gunton is in favour of a return to God as 'the one' and disagrees with those who think this God will stifle 'the many', enslaving humanity and demeaning the world in ways which we have seen give rise to atheism. The Trinity is just the God we need to make liberation possible, according to Gunton, who emphasizes the genuine differentness of the divine persons, their substantiality, yet highlights equally their mutual interpenetration, employing the traditional term *perichoresis*, all of which issues in a genuine relationality of the divine persons. Thus in the life of God 'the one' and 'the many' are in proper relationship. And so it can be in the world, according to Gunton, where inspired by such a fundamental vision of God, humanity might be liberated from oppressive dominance of 'the one' and of 'the many', in the various disordered forms these distortions appear, to find peace with itself and with the natural environment.

While the Trinity has often been seen in hierarchical terms, with the priority of the divine Father reinforcing the remoteness of God typical of classical theism, nevertheless it is everywhere reclaimed and reminted nowadays as a critique of such oppressive and disconnected God-images. The concepts and images of panentheism examined in this chapter are fully compatible with Trinitarian imagery. Indeed, the Trinity is the classic attempt of the Church to conceive of God as both transcendent and immanent. It stands behind other more recent images, and supports them. In the prophetic critique of Colin Gunton, we see that the God of classical theism sidelined by modern atheism has been replaced by a variety of oppressive unifying principles which have helped distort the properly relational nature of humanity and the world. The Trinity, however, provides a view of God which does not dishonour the rich particularity of people and indeed of all created entities, but powerfully evokes their relatedness. This is just the sort of God-image we have been seeking.

The task for our next three chapters is to begin investigating how a God found 'in, with and under' the life of the world, though not exhausted by the life of the world, might be understood to act in the life of that world.

Notes

1 See the highly instructive diagram in John Macquarrie, *Principles of Christian Theology* (rev. edn; London: SCM, 1977), p. 167.

2 John Macquarrie, *In Search of Deity: An Essay in Dialectical Theism* (London: SCM, 1984).

3 John A. T. Robinson, *Truth is Two-Eyed* (London: SCM, 1979), p. 29.

4 Macquarrie, *In Search*, pp. 172–82.

5 *Ibid.*, p. 181.

6 Kosuke Koyama, *Three Mile an Hour God* (London: SCM, 1979).

7 Macquarrie, *In Search*, pp. 22–6.

8 Sallie McFague, *Models of God: Theology for an Ecological, Nuclear Age* (Philadelphia: Fortress, 1987), pp. 35, 39.

9 *Ibid.*, p. 61.

10 Grace Jantzen, *God's World, God's Body* (Philadelphia: Westminster, 1984).

11 *Ibid.*, p. 34.

12 *Ibid.*, p. 83.

13 McFague, *Models*, pp. 75–8.

14 *Ibid.*, p. 71.

15 Jantzen, *God's World*, p. 127.

16 John Polkinghorne, *Science and Providence: God's Interaction with the World* (London: SPCK, 1989), pp. 18–23, p. 23; for the Gaia hypothesis, see James Lovelock, *Gaia* (Oxford: Oxford University Press, 1979).

17 Gerard Manley Hopkins, 'God's Grandeur', *Poems and Prose* (London: Penguin, 1953), p. 27.

18 McFague, *Models*, p. 63.

19 *Ibid.*, pp. 82–83.

20 *Ibid.*, pp. 97–123.

21 Arthur Peacocke, *Creation and the World of Science* (Oxford: Clarendon, 1979), p. 142.

22 Anna Case-Winters, *God's Power: Traditional Understandings and Contemporary Challenges* (Louisville, KY: Westminster John Knox, 1990), p. 225.

23 *Ibid.*, p. 222.

24 Jantzen, *God's World*, p. 130.

25 Norman Pittenger, *Picturing God* (London: SCM, 1982).

26 McFague, *In Search*, p. 128.

27 *Ibid.*, p. 133.

28 *Ibid.*, pp. 157–80.

29 Frans Josef van Beeck SJ, *God Proclaimed: A Contemporary Catholic Systematic Theology*, Vol. 2, Intro. and Pt 1 (Minneapolis, MN: Michael Glazier, 1993), p. 311.

30 Peter Armstrong, 'Television as a medium for theology', in Peter Eaton (ed.), *The Trial of Faith: Theology and the Church Today* (Worthing: Churchman, 1988), pp. 183–93, p. 190.

31 Note that this discussion reflects trends within the Western Church. The Eastern Orthodox trend is toward understanding God's relationship with the world in terms of 'uncreated energies', a doctrine championed most significantly by Gregory Palamas, a fourteenth-century Archbishop of Thessalonika. It tempers Western emphasis on God's direct embrace of the world: see, e.g. Vladimir Lossky, *The Mystical Theology of the Eastern Church* (1944, ET 1957) (Cambridge: James Clarke, 1973), pp. 67–90. My St Barnabas' colleague, Duncan Reid, has done a most significant ecumenical study bringing leading recent exponents of Eastern and Western thinking on the Trinity into fruitful dialogue: see his *Energies of the Spirit: Trinitarian Models in Eastern Orthodox and Western Theology* (American Academy of Religion Academy Series 96; Atlanta, GA: Scholars Press, 1997); on East, West and this idea of God indwelling the world, see especially pp. 104–9.

32 It is a mark of Macquarrie's conceptual approach here that he did not consider the mystical tradition. Because, in the midst of much Platonic dualism such as that characterizing the influential, anonymous fourteenth-century work *The Cloud of Unknowing*, there are figures like Julian of Norwich and Hildegard of Bingen who stand as witnesses to a more holistic view of God.

33 John Macquarrie, *In Search*, pp. 72–84, 78–9.

34 *Ibid.*, pp. 98–110, p. 109.

35 *Ibid.*, pp. 111–24.

36 *Ibid.*, pp. 139–52, p. 150.

37 Thomas Aquinas, *Summa theologiae*, 1a.3, cited in Placher *The Domestication of Transcendence: How Modern Thinking about God Went Wrong* (Louisville, KY: Westminster John Knox, 1996), p. 21.

38 *Summa theologiae*, 1a.13.3 ad 1, cited in Placher, *Domestication*, p. 30.

39 Placher, *Domestication*, p. 31.

40 *Summa theologiae*, 2a.2ae.2.9, cited in Placher, *Domestication*, p. 33.

41 See also the sensitive discussion in Frans Josef van Beeck, *God Encountered: A Contemporary Catholic Systematic Theology*, Vol. 2, Pt 2, Ch. 10, in which Anselm as well as Aquinas is presented not as a rationalist but as a theologian open to the mystery of God discerned in the dynamics of Christian faith and worship, yet

calling reason into theology's service. For Aquinas, according to van Beeck, it is faith that prompts reason to interpret God's world. In a long discussion of the five ways, from the first part of Aquinas' *Summa*, van Beeck agrees with Placher that this is anything but the rational proof of God it is often taken to be in the light of Scholastic rationalism. He then offers a useful account of the rise and fall of this rationalistic reading, up to Vatican II.

42 Martin Luther, *Lectures on Hebrews*, in *Luther's Works*, Vol. 29 (St Louis, MO: Concordia, 1968), p. 111, cited in Placher, *Domestication*, p. 47.

43 John Calvin, *Congregation on Eternal Election*, in Philip C. Holtrup, *The Bolsec Controversy on Predestination from 1551 to 1555*, Vol. 1, Bk 2 (Lewiston, NY: Edwin Mellon, 1993), p. 717, cited in Placher, *Domestication*, p. 66.

44 Catherine Mowry LaCugna, *God For Us: The Trinity and Christian Life* (1991) (New York: HarperCollins, 1993), p. 10; all of Pt 1 is relevant here.

45 Karl Rahner SJ, *The Trinity* (1967, ET 1970) (New York: Crossroad, 1997), pp. 10–11.

46 John Calvin, *Institutes of the Christian Religion* (1536) (Philadelphia: Westminster, 1960), 1.13.2, cited in Placher, *Domestication*, pp. 166–7.

47 Placher, *Domestication*, pp. 174–8.

48 Colin Gunton, *The One, the Three and the Many: God, Creation and the Culture of Modernity* (Cambridge: Cambridge University Press, 1993), p. 145; see also a stimulating discussion of the Trinity as the Christian form of belief in God beyond theism and atheism in Walter Kasper, *The God of Jesus Christ* (1982) (London: SCM, 1984).

49 Macquarrie, *Principles*, pp. 198–202.

50 Leonardo Boff, *Trinity and Society* (Maryknoll, NY: Orbis, 1988).

51 Moltmann himself points this out, so there can be no doubt! See 'An open letter to José Míguez Bonino', *Christianity and Crisis*, **36** (1976), pp. 57–63.

52 Jürgen Moltmann, *The Crucified God: The Cross of Christ as the Foundation and Criticism of Christian Theology* (1973) (London: SCM, 1974), p. 227.

53 *Ibid.*, p. 277.

54 Jürgen Moltmann, *The Trinity and the Kingdom of God: The Doctrine of God* (1980) (London: SCM, 1981), p. 83.

55 Gunton, *The One*.

56 Fredric Jameson, *Postmodernism, or, the Cultural Logic of Late Capitalism* (London: Verso, 1991).

57 David Harvey, *The Condition of Postmodernity: An Inquiry into the Origins of Cultural Change* (Oxford: Blackwell, 1990).

Part II

At Work in the World?

4 Divine Action: Classic Themes

. . . not so much a force being exercised as an infinite goodness being communicated. Love is the unfathomable source of all causality.

Etienne Gilson, *The Christian Philosophy of St Thomas Aquinas*, 1956

The spacious firmament on high,
With all the blue ethereal sky,
And spangled heavens, a shining frame,
Their great Original proclaim.

Joseph Addison (1672–1719) 'The Spacious Firmament on High'

And I have felt
A presence that disturbs me with the joy
Of elevated thoughts; a sense sublime
Of something far more deeply interfused,
Whose dwelling is the light of setting suns,
And the round ocean, and the living air,
And the blue sky, and in the mind of man

William Wordsworth (1770–1850) 'Tintern Abbey'

God breathes within the confines
of our definition of him, agonising
over immensities that will not return

R. S. Thomas (1913–   ) 'The White Tiger'

Now we acquaint ourselves with some key ways in which God's action has been conceived. We take particular note of the 'double agency' tradition, which received its classic formulation from Thomas Aquinas, but is already recognizable in the Hebrew Scriptures, and remains so in much of today's liberal theology. This approach expresses an abiding conviction of Judaeo-Christian imagination, that God is Lord of the cosmos as a whole and all its parts, but also a God who honours the integrity of creation and delights in all creatures living and acting according to their particular natures. This is a paradox, to be sure, of God at work in a world which is itself at work. It reminds us we are not limited to the religiously barren theology of a remote God intervening in a closed world – an account which has unfortunately become widespread since the seventeenth century.

This chapter will unfold in three sections, setting out these themes. First, we trace the emergence of double agency as the main pre-modern account of divine action. This is a resilient tradition, and we later see it maintaining a presence at the Enlightenment and reasserting itself in more recent discussion. Second, we investigate the modern emergence of belief that our world is a closed, natural order, first mechanical and then evolutionary, with profound but varied implications for understanding divine action. These developments challenge but also provide resources for reinventing the double agency tradition. Then we take our third step, considering some liberal approaches in the wake of Schleiermacher, along with Barth and Bultmann, identifying issues for a discussion of how the question of divine action might best be approached today, to follow in subsequent chapters.

Pre-modernity and double agency

According to double agency, the forces of nature, the creatures of the Earth and human beings are all at work, and the world's life takes shape through this ceaseless activity. Yet God is at work, too, in all these actions. But God does not represent one cause among others, as process theology suggests, its God contributing to every event, nor the only cause of all events, as we saw to be the case for Malebranche in Chapter 2, above, whose world-suppressing theology in the seventeenth century helped spawn atheism (thus proving the rule that God is not exalted by the demeaning of God's creatures). The solidification of this resilient tradition of double agency in the patristic era and its continuance into the present will be important to trace, but first I shall consider the suggestion that its roots are in the Bible, as also in Christian experience.

Double agency and the Bible

Various strata in the Hebrew Scriptures testify to both nature and history as the arenas of God's activity, yet at the same time they are the means by which life unfolds through natural and human agency. Some key examples from the great epic narratives of creation and redemption will suffice to make the point.

God's creation in Genesis enlists the help of creatures, who carry forward God's purpose by their own fruitfulness, filling the Earth and, in the case of humans, subduing it.[1] The care of God for Israel is demonstrated through the troubled human relations of the Joseph story which nevertheless express God's action.[2] The Exodus account sees God at work in the stubbornness of Pharaoh and in savage plagues of natural pestilence,[3] in the strong East wind and in the maelstrom of the Red Sea.[4] The settlement of the promised land is affected by numerous battles[5] where humans do the fighting but God wins the victory – 'not because of the strength and power of man and of the horse', as Martin Luther explains, reflecting the same view, 'but under the veil and covering of man and of the horse [God] fights and does all'.[6] The restoration from exile in Babylon represents God's providential guidance of historical events,[7] just as the exile itself was understood as God's judgement.[8] There are also many instances in the Hebrew Scriptures of God taking firm control of the world and of human beings. There are the inspired utterance and miraculous powers of prophets, for instance, where miracles are God-disclosing events defying the normal natural patterns which ancient civilizations knew, though in prescientific ways.

But here there is no modern problem of a closed natural and historical order into which God intervenes from outside. As William Placher puts it, 'Divine action is not an interruption in or a violation of the normal course of things, but precisely is the normal course of things.'[9] Placher points out that there are parts of the Hebrew Scriptures where events unfold with little special action of God, as in the narrative history of King David, while others are full of wonders, like the Elijah cycle,[10] but between these accounts there is no sense of development, with both types pointing to the action of God for Israel, albeit in different ways.[11] So it is God's world, and if God is able to do extraordinary, inexplicable things in it, God is also at work through ordinary natural and human activity. Psalm 104 is a classic statement of this, with imagery of a remote God watering the Earth from on high to cause growth, alongside images of God more intimately involved in care for God's creatures:

> These all look to you
>> to give them their food in due season;
> when you give to them, they gather it up;
>> when you open your hand, they are filled with good things.
> When you hide your face, they are dismayed;
>> when you take away their breath, they die and return to their dust.
> When you send forth your spirit, they are created;
>> and you renew the face of the ground.[12]

The Hebrew Scriptures are marked by polemic against nature religion among the nations Israel encountered, which makes the transcendent God of Israel theologically distinctive.[13] But transcendence does not mean remoteness. For the Hebrew Scriptures, God is of an order greater in every way than the world, while nevertheless embracing, infusing and empowering the world, as much from within as from without.

In the New Testament the paradox manifest in talk of double agency may appear to be less in evidence, with the power of God over nature and human beings asserted again and again. There are nature miracles in the Gospels,[14] and an elevated conception of Christian life as an existence beyond death, sin and social convention. This all serves to emphasize that the Christ event is a God event – it was the burden of New Testament writers to establish and commend this. But the Christ event is also a natural and a human event. Jesus is portrayed using illustrations for divine truths, and means for revelatory action, drawn from the life of the world, like saliva in healing, water in foot washing and bread and wine for the sacrament of his continuing presence. Indeed, the fact that the 'Son of Man', 'the human one', Jesus of Nazareth, is presented as the very presence of God in the New Testament represents the classic instance of double agency, which centuries later at the Council of Chalcedon (AD 451) received its definitive expression: Christ is one person with two natures, one divine and the other human, united 'without confusion, change, division or separation'. Here is God at work and a human being at work in perfect accord; here is God fully at home in a human life. As other approaches to divine action might deny the significance of the world, or else marginalize the role of God, so in the early Church some limited the significance of Jesus' humanity (Apollinarianism), while others limited the significance of God in accounting for Jesus (Adoptionism).[15] But in the doctrine of Christ's incarnation the double agency view is demonstrated in all its paradoxicality, emerging from a biblical vision of God at work in the work of God's world and of God's chosen people.

Double agency and Christian experience

The biblical witness resonates with the experience of Christians ancient and modern. In particular, the double agency paradox of Christ's incarnation is correlated with the paradoxical experience of double agency typically characteristic of Christian life. 'By the grace of God I am what I am,' Paul declares, ' . . . I worked harder than any of them – though it was not I, but the grace of God that is with me.'[16] This conviction, repeated in various forms by all the saints, is called 'the paradox of grace' by D. M. Baillie in a classic Christological essay of the last generation. He writes,

> This is a highly paradoxical conviction, for in ascribing all to God it does not abrogate human personality nor disclaim personal responsibility. Never is human action more truly and fully personal, never does the agent feel more perfectly free, than in those moments of which he can say as a Christian that whatever good was in them was not his but God's.[17]

This sense of being God's instrument in particular situations is a genuine, if not constant, experience of Christian clergy and laity in the practice of ministry. I daresay it is psychologically parallel to the experiences of an artist or writer in the grip of inspiration, or of anyone possessed of a resolute conviction that drives them to action. Yet these are not cases of possession where a brainwashed individual functions unconsciously as the instrument of an overmastering force. Rather, it is an experience of exhilarating synchrony, in which a fully conscious acting person is nevertheless aware that the action, while his or her own, is also God's action. It is not a sense of God helping, of being a part of the action, but of God performing the action while at the same time the acting person performs it. In this way, as in the biblical illustrations offered, we discern a Christian paradox of double agency. How has that tradition of understanding God's action taken shape?

The double agency tradition

Among the second- and third-century apologists, Irenaeus insists that God deals gently not intrusively with the world, at home in the world as a creator who 'does not need to break and enter, being immanent',[18] while for Origen God respects the world's integrity as it develops toward its completion – a completion which involves the enfleshed divine Logos. Gregory of Nyssa, in the subsequent age of the Creeds, conceives of God permeating creation and holding it in being, relating to each creature according to its nature, which van Beeck rightly points out is a far cry from intervening deities of the ancient pantheon.[19] This non-interventionist, double agency reading of the Fathers is also characteristic of Augustine, for whom 'On the one hand the divine sovereignty, decree and providence reign absolutely over all history, and God controls all creaturely action', while 'On the other hand, God does not act as a finite cause but in and through finite causes, natural and human' and, if *outside* the visible world, then only 'through the mediation of *other finite things*, especially the angels'.[20]

Albert the Great, Master of Thomas Aquinas, was a keen student of nature.[21] And in his famous pupil we have a theologian eager to honour the created natures of all things, letting them follow their nature to its proper ends. His approach was to combine Aristotle, whose God was an external cause of things, with Neoplatonism, where God is the ultimate form in which all finite things participate.[22] 'Using Aristotle's distinction of four causes, material, final, efficient, and formal, Thomas explains how God is the source of all material causes, the goal of all action, the first cause of all agents, and the source of all forms.'[23] Particular events are the work of primary (God) and secondary (natural) agency together, by analogy with the artisan and the tool, both of which contribute to the wood being split, the nail being driven, etc. These are actions performed wholly by God and wholly by the secondary agent, though on different levels.[24] This is not to say that two actions work side by side, like two people carrying a load. This would misunderstand God to be 'a cause like other causes, differing only in power, a demiurge. . . . So considered, God's intervention would overrule all secondary causes, and thus deprive them of their natural action; hence there would no longer be any contingency, chance, or freedom.'[25]

It is true that God for Aquinas can act apart from the normal order of the world and produce the results of secondary causes without them or surpassing them,[26] but this is not to deny the overall force of his more general dictum '*detrahere actiones proprias robus est divinae bonitati derogare*': 'to deprive things of actions of their own is to belittle God's goodness'. Etienne Gilson, who cites the dictum, is eager to present this view of divine action as a profoundly Christian philosophy based on God's great love for creation, rather than the rationalistic product it became in the hands of later neo-Thomism (as we noted in Chapter 2, above) – 'If no philosophy was so constantly busy safeguarding the rights of creatures,' Gilson concludes, 'it is because (Aquinas) saw in this the one means of safeguarding the rights of God.'[27]

The Reformation did not significantly alter the double agency theology. Although Calvin (and Barth after him) insisted on the absolute primacy of God's action, nevertheless secondary causes were real. While Calvin's God governed every drop of rain and every bird's flight, nevertheless God is not directly responsible for evil, which is the responsibility of secondary causes.[28] Calvin invoked a paradox of predestination to explain how even evil acts could be in God's predestined plan for the world though God is in no way responsible for their execution by free agents; Luther declared that Judas became a traitor by his own will, which was nevertheless also God's invincible will. Neither claimed to understand how this could be.[29] The Lutheran Scholastic J. A. Quenstedt (1617–1680) declared of all phenomena that the same effect is produced 'not by God alone, nor by the creature alone, nor partly by God and partly by the creature, but at the same time by God and the creature'.[30] And so it was until the rise of science in the seventeenth century. As Austin Farrer correctly observed, 'Metaphysics remained rooted in physics, and the Aristotelian account of physical causes was the most serviceable to be had until Galileo and Newton displaced it.'[31] And it is to this displacement we now turn, with its profound consequences for the understanding of God's action in the world.

Modernity and the crisis of divine action

God and mechanistic science

The medieval world saw God at work in formal and final as well as efficient causes, as the transcendent impulse immanent in all of them. The reduction of all causality to efficient causality in scientific method from the sixteenth century led to the problem of God in a world of mechanistic science in the seventeenth century. For this shift we can thank Galileo (1564–1642), who inherited the religious and aesthetic mood of Copernicus and Kepler with their powerful mathematical appreciation of planetary motion and added to it the practice of experimentation. He sought to check conventional opinions by experiment, as well as his own new theories. This was not an atheistic undertaking for Galileo, nor for most seventeenth-century scientists. But it was disruptive of a religious world-view based on purpose, leaving a world of particles in motion in the hands of a science of descriptions.[32]

The world had been one in which social and cosmic orders mirrored one another; the world had been read allegorically as speaking of divine purpose and human utility. Michel Foucault provides an excellent example based on comparison of a sixteenth-century bestiary with a seventeenth-century one. Aldrovandi's *History of Serpents and Dragons*, of the sixteenth century, gives allegorical significance as well as anatomy for the animals portrayed, not to mention instructions for their capture and cooking! While in Johnston's *Natural History of Quadrupeds*, from 1657, the tenor of modern science is evident, abstracting creatures from the realm of human meaning and presenting them 'objectively' in terms of name, anatomy and habitat only.[33] Instead of a metaphorical cosmos we discover a mathematical one – Descartes' geometric universe filled with extended bodies. And Newton explained the dynamics of these extended bodies as no one before, with a theory of universal gravitation that stunned the age by its mathematical power and straightforward mechanistic audacity.

How to make religious sense in the new environment, and to conceive God at work in it? Seventeenth-century science remained a religious activity, with much 'goodwill toward orthodoxy' among the 'Virtuosi', the English scientists of the day, and the theological interpreters of a new world they were elucidating. They resisted the atheistic materialism we have seen emerging in Diderot and d'Holbach, and even earlier in England with Thomas Hobbes (1588–1679). And they resisted the pantheism of Baruch Spinoza (1632–1677) who had rejected Cartesian dualism in favour of a single universal substance, a God he equated with the newly discovered inexorable laws of nature. In the physicists Robert Boyle and Isaac Newton there was still a belief that God held the universe in being, and was sustaining its regularities. But Leibniz, Newton's opponent, was unimpressed with the creator of a universe that could not stand entirely on its own, for Newton's universe still needed occasional divine correction, whereas Leibniz's God had created 'the best of all possible worlds', not needing such divine sustenance to keep it in being. Finally, when the mathematician Laplace famously accounted for the anomalies in planetary motion which Newton's celestial mechanics had failed to explain, and the orbits of planets became a regular, self-correcting clockwork for the first time, the God hypothesis was no longer needed to keep the universe in being. As Ian Barbour put it, 'Divine preservation started as active sustenance, became passive acquiescence, and was then forgotten',[34] and the God which Barbour called 'the cosmic plumber', the ultimate conservative fixing leaks in the system, could be retired. Here we have a major turning point in the way Western humanity understood its world and God's action within it, with the completion of Newton's mathematical account. It was a very different world from the medieval one. It was a view of the cosmos which saw in man a puny, irrelevant spectator of the vast mathematical system whose regular motions according to mechanical principles constituted the world of nature. . . . The world that people had thought themselves living in – a world rich with colour and sound, redolent with fragrance, filled with gladness, love and beauty, speaking everywhere of purposive harmony and creative ideals – was crowded now into minute corners in the brains of scattered organic beings. The really important world outside was a world hard, cold, colourless, silent, and dead. . . . In Newton the Cartesian metaphysics . . . finally overthrew Aristotelianism and became the predominant world-view of modern times.[35]

From this new perspective came a new way of understanding God's action, which remains well represented in Christian sensibility today. And that is the notion of God intervening in an otherwise independent world. How else is God to operate if the world is a closed order of rigid law, but to intervene regally from time to time? Divine intervention was denied by and large in deism, while its defence became the orthodox riposte against deism. Deists tended to close the universe to divine intervention, apart from an initial creation which set up conditions for the natural unfolding of things by self-consistent laws.[36] Joseph Glanville and Walter Charleton were among the seventeenth-century English theologians who resisted deism by claiming divine intervention, while Ralph Cudworth thought that God sometimes appears as a character in his own drama[37] (a notion, I might add, recalling the classical deus ex machina, who was a familiar character in baroque opera of the day, lowered by ropes to the music of recorders).

But, as I say, not everyone was open to the notion of divine intervention. An early eighteenth-century deist, Thomas Woolston, queried miracles as forgeries.[38] The best-known proponent of this scepticism is of course the radical empiricist David Hume (1711–1776). The regularities of nature attested by long and diverse human experience strike Hume as sufficiently weighty to deny all claims to a miracle contravening such observed regularities. In Hume's own words,

> there is not to be found, in all history, any miracle attested by a sufficient number of men, of such unquestioned good sense, education and learning, as to secure us against all delusion in themselves; of such undoubted integrity, as to place them beyond all suspicion of any design to deceive others; of such credit and reputation in the eyes of mankind, as to have a great deal to lose in the case of their being detected in any falsehood; and at the same time, attesting facts performed in such a public manner and in so celebrated a part of the world, as to render the detection unavoidable: All which circumstances are requisite to give us a full assurance in the testimony of men.[39]

All of this is a wholly new way of understanding God's action in the world, whether or not you believed divine intervention took place. In a pre-modern context miracle is not about divine intervention; rather, 'in a world where God sustains everything at every moment, what distinguishes miracle is our inability to understand their causes and the wonder that results, not the fact that God acts in them and not elsewhere.'[40] As William Placher sums it up, 'the Deists posited a God who created everything and then stepped out of the picture, while their opponents invented a God who jumped in and out of creation in a way earlier theologians would not have recognised.'[41]

God and a world of change

But our story does not end there, with the world left in the hands of empiricists and rationalists. The Romantic movement in the late eighteenth century turned on its Enlightenment parents, reasserting intuition in the face of reason, and feeling in the face of empiricism. 'The divine indwelling, God's immanence in the world and in the human soul, which had been lost in Deism, was reasserted by the romantic poets.'[42] And immanentist conceptions of God were given great impetus in the extraordinary intellectual upheaval of the nineteenth century, which centred on historicism and evolutionism. In other words, change was discovered as the core principle of metaphysics, rather than stasis, which had predominated in the Western view of reality since Plato.

Natural history began to register new facts in geology and biology which called into question the accepted ideas of our Earth as a recent planet, and the fixity of species upon it. At last, in the theoretical tour de force achieved by Charles Darwin (1809–1882), an idea of profound simplicity became the basis of modern biology, with implications for how we understand history, society and theology. Evolution by natural selection from among advantageous mutations is a powerful and elegant way to account for an extraordinary amount of data in the biological sciences. How could one be a deist any more, if there was no original creation in which we still lived, but rather an ongoing process of geological change and natural evolution? Ours is no longer the world as it had been at the start, when deism believed God had created it complete and entire.

With evolution in biology and, in the same decade, the discovery of the electromagnetic field and its mathematical elucidation in six elegant differential equations by James Clerk Maxwell; with the historical idealism of Hegel, and the fruit of a century of historical study of the Scriptures as testimony to developing human understanding of God; with Romanticism and its 'sense sublime Of something far more deeply interfused',[43] the situation was ripe for reconceiving God in the wake of static, seventeenth-century clockwork imagery. How was this challenge met in theology?

Beginning to rethink divine action

We turn now to three trends in nineteenth- and twentieth-century theology that dealt with this new environment in various ways, before going on to consider more recent, holistically inspired options for again thinking divine action 'in, with and under' the world process, in subsequent chapters. The three options we consider for now are a version of double agency in Schleiermacher and his followers, but without divine intervention, then another liberal view that allowed some divine intervention in the process, recalling Newton, and finally the challenges of Barth and Bultmann to the whole way the divine action issue has been set up in modernity.

Liberal theology and uniform divine action

Owen Thomas, in a helpful historical overview of approaches to divine action in the world, observes that 'the liberal view ... was merely a simplified form of the traditional doctrine of primary and secondary causes with miracles deleted'.[44] This was certainly the case with Friedrich Schleiermacher (1768–1834), the father of modern liberal theology.[45] Schleiermacher holds creation and providence together in a developmental vision of continuous creation, with God active in every event of every causal series, not simply as the absentee God of deism content to bequeath to us a first cause. He reclaims the tradition of primary and secondary causation, using the image of horizontal causality from within the world system and vertical causality from God, both accounting fully for all that happens. It is important for Schleiermacher that these two causal orders are kept distinct, ensuring that theology and science are never in conflict, which is always the case when divine action is understood as abnormal intervention from 'outside', not to mention ensuring that God is not reduced to one cause among others. Schleiermacher's commitment to 'the metaphysical uniformity of divine action'[46] excludes special divine action, even in the person of Jesus, whose uniquely potent God-consciousness is not achieved by miracle, arising rather as an example of God's normal engagement with all humanity. Regardless of which special revelations and divine acts are claimed, what they really tell us about are the perceptions of those who claim them, who have a heightened sense of God's unvarying presence and activity in those events. But that is all. 'Miracle is simply the religious name for event',[47] Schleiermacher tells the 'cultured despisers of religion'.

This is a view echoed by more recent liberal followers of Schleiermacher. Maurice Wiles, an important late twentieth-century contributor to the divine action debate, also champions uniform divine action, miracle as a matter of perception and an adoptionist Christology, so Jesus can be understood as emerging naturally from nature and history without special divine involvement. Wiles wants to say that God acts in the world, but not in a way that interferes with natural processes, so he concludes that the whole natural process, the world making itself through natural history and human history, is one single divine act.[48] John Hick, a fellow contributor with Wiles to a controversial volume *The Myth of God Incarnate*, which finally brought such thinking home to English theology as late as 1977, insists with Schleiermacher on the primacy of religious experience in grounding belief in God. Accordingly, miracle is a matter of perception, of the ordinary experienced as extraordinary, from the defeat of the Amelekites in which an historical event is interpreted as miraculous intervention, to a faster-than-expected flight home across the Atlantic interpreted as a divine blessing, while for those flying against it the same wind that sped you home becomes an obstacle and an irritation.[49] Of such perspectives, Barbour is right to conclude that 'Liberal theologians, and those traditionalists who accepted evolution, preserved the classical understanding of God, but now spoke of him as working continuously through the whole evolutionary process by means of secondary causes.'[50]

Liberal theology and special divine action

Other liberals who follow this approach show a greater willingness to speak about special divine action within the weft of natural happenings. Gordon Kaufman shares with Wiles an understanding of all cosmic, natural and human history as a single divine act, but allows within it various 'subacts' whereby God directs the process. So things we might want to see as subject to special divine guidance, such as the course taken by the cosmos and the evolution of life at particular key junctures, or the emergence of humanity and its salvation history, can be seen as subacts of the single overarching act of God, not interventions but unfoldings of the plan. Clearly there is a limit to how close this model of God can get to the providential God of much popular belief. Kaufman admits that there is no way one could say of this God that 'He walks with me and he talks with me'; his is a grand, even austere vision with little space for pious sentiment concerning divine action on our behalf. The bracing inexorability of the cross is one indicator for Kaufman that God is more interested in the big picture than in offering comfort on a human scale, (whereas for Moltmann, of course, the cross is good news for every victim of a crucifying world).[51]

A similar liberal approach is taken by G. Ernest Wright (1909–1974) in mid-twentieth-century biblical theology, though it is not always identified as such. Wright wishes to emphasize the objectivity of divine action against the view that it is simply a matter of interior perception, as in Schleiermacher and later liberals. He knows that the Bible is about a divine actor, in both Testaments, and proclaims the *magnalia dei*, the mighty acts of God, as the Bible's key theme.[52] But this apparent anti-liberal agenda is conducted by veiled liberal means. The mighty acts are not those we read about in the Bible, such as wonders accompanying the Exodus, but natural and historical events which stood behind the narratives and were elaborated into the grand miracles that appear in Scripture. Here is the liberal belief that God works in normal events of normal history, but with their status as objective divine acts strenuously affirmed none the less. These historical events, behind the text, are the acts of deliverance by God.

It was Langdon Gilkey who pointed out the obvious here,[53] that such modern liberal reassertion of special divine action reads the miracle accounts analogically rather than literally, and univocally, hence departing from pre-modern belief in full-scale, nature-changing divine actions. But it is not a new strategy. In liberal biblical scholarship of the nineteenth century, cataclysmic divine actions were regularly reinterpreted as divine acts cloaked in fortuitous bits of weather, just as miracles of Jesus were reclothed as perfectly explicable events albeit full of valuable divine teaching, which were later elaborated into supernatural accounts. But rather than inventing (historical) sandbanks just under the water upon which Jesus (miraculously) walked, or proposing (naturally explicable) relief from psychopathology behind (miraculous) cures by Jesus, the only history we can reliably point to in many such cases is the historical reality of faith in the early Church, which is expressed through stories such as these, often with conscious use of analogy. We do not have to invent 'normal' history to stand behind these narratives, and then interpret it as special divine action.

Karl Barth and Rudolf Bultmann

No one could be less liberal than Karl Barth (1886–1968), who represents a totally different approach to the matter in hand. He conceives God differently from liberals who are religiously concerned to accommodate God's action with a scientific view of natural causes. His God is Lord and Sovereign, and acts just as Calvin's predestining God acts, doing everything, though through secondary means. Of special interest here is the thin account of scientific law we find in Barth, who grants such laws strictly limited validity. Such laws are pointers to a fuller law that we cannot know, the law of God's actual working in the world. And while such laws are signs that God is constant and faithful, rather than capricious, nevertheless it is very important for Barth that

> we cannot hypostasise the concept of law, as though in our dealings with it we really had to do with the ruling representative and vice-gerent of God. ... We have to do directly with God, and only indirectly with the laws, so far as they are known to us. It is God Himself, in fact, who is the law of all occurrence.[54]

And in this vein Barth goes on to justify divine action in the form of miracle. Though it is not the suspension of natural law of which he speaks, but rather appearances through the thin veil of natural law as we construe it of that real law governing the universe, which is God. Barth writes,

Naturally there can be no question of His contravening or overturning any real or ontic law of creaturely occurrence. This would mean that He was not at unity with Himself in His will and work. But we must allow that He can ruthlessly ignore the laws known to us, that is, our own perception of the ontic laws of creaturely occurrence. Even then, God does not act as a god of disorder, but as the God of His own order, who precedes creaturely occurrence even in the fact that He is not bound by our human concepts of order, however great may be the noetic clarity and certainty which we believe them to possess.[55]

With the Schleiermacher tradition in theological liberalism, Rudolf Bultmann (1884–1976) believed that faith in the perceiver is an essential part of properly confessing divine action. With Barth he insists that a proper understanding of divine action is not about speculative links between God and natural processes as we understand them. Bultmann also recognizes the big problem Wright and others make for themselves, with possible historical disconfirmation of the very historical events they postulate. Bultmann holds a double agency view, though he refuses to objectify the divine action which in faith he confesses. For Bultmann,

The only way to preserve the unworldly, transcendental character of the divine activity is to regard it not as an interference in worldly happenings, but something accomplished in them in such a way that the closed weft of history as it presents itself to objective observation is left undisturbed. To every other eye than the eye of faith the action of God is hidden. Only the 'natural' happening is generally visible and ascertainable. In it is accomplished the hidden act of God.[56]

So what to do with the accounts of God acting on the stage of history in the Bible? We have seen what Wright does with them, interpreting them as veiled history. For Bultmann, by contrast, such accounts need to be 'demythologized', which means reinterpreted existentially. 'God as acting does not refer to an event which can be perceived by me without myself being drawn into the event as into God's action,'[57] Bultmann insists. For example, to affirm that God is creator is nothing to do with how the world came into being, but can only be a personal confession that we understand ourselves to be creatures which owe their existence to God. It cannot be a neutral statement, but only one of thanksgiving and surrender. For Bultmann, mythological language of a publicly acting God is dangerous for theology because it risks scientific and historical challenge, but also because it improperly objectifies God.

An assessment of modern trends

The impact of modernity brought an end to the world as it was imagined before mechanistic physics and, later, evolutionary biology made it self-contained and self-perpetuating. Instead of God's world, and our home, our symbolically friendly abode of meaning, it became an engine, then an organism, raising questions about how God might be thought alongside this world, and we too, who once knew our place in it, however tenuous.

According to liberal theology God is at work in the world process, which in pre-modernity was static and hierarchical, but is now dynamic and temporal. We also find a resurgence of the double agency tradition – the liberal God is at work through secondary causes. For some liberals, such as Schleiermacher, Wiles and Hick, divine action is uniform and anything exceptional or revelatory is simply a matter of perspective, of the ordinary perceived as extraordinary. For others, such as Kaufman and Wright, there is room for special divine action at grand junctions in cosmic and salvation history, of course through secondary causes. How do these trends fare under examination?

In all these recent liberals we find a serious engagement with emerging views of the world as an evolving system, and an attempt to explain the Christian sense that particular events seem providential and revelatory. But this is a big-picture God, a God of nature and history – not a God who can conceivably care for the widow and the fatherless, for the stranger in the land, for the least of these little ones, for the sparrow that falls. A commendable job with modern science has not been matched here by a commendable job in the interpretation of biblical faith. This God is too big and important and cosmic to be concerned for and involved with individuals, be they human or animal. This is not a God who will encourage, enliven, comfort, warn, divert or rescue, unless it is by systemic factors that all could feel and benefit from if properly attuned.

Regardless of whether there is room for a special action of God, or if there is room for it only on really major occasions, nevertheless the nature of God's sustaining and supportive role behind the cosmos as a whole is not clear in these accounts. The question of how God is at work, in one great act or in many subacts, is an important one. Could it be that all that these liberals are doing is asserting God's involvement as a matter of faith, having come to believe in God on the basis of design arguments, or religious experience? But if it is not clear how God is related to the world as they conceive it, then the risk is well established that the world might come readily to be atheistically conceived. We explored this development in Chapter 2, with the mechanistic, seventeenth-century world in view. We have also seen God banished from the more recent evolutionary world of biology by atheists such as Richard Dawkins, for whom talk of God at work in the evolutionary process would be poetry at best, and dangerously misleading nonsense at worst.

What is clear in all these liberals, however, is that divine action, if unclear in the world, is nevertheless perceived in human minds and operative in human experiences. But in Chapter 2 we also saw that leaving the world to science and seeking God in the human self was no great success either.

The double agency tradition is also present in Barth and Bultmann. But they differ from the liberals in their assessment of modernity and its closed natural order. Both are Kantian and dualistic in their approach. The human being is excerpted from the world of which it is a part. For both, the natural world is a shadowy backdrop for the drama of human salvation. And these approaches too, not just those of the liberals we have considered, are problematic.

It has been pointed out that the evolutionary conception of the world in later modernity is less prominent in neo-orthodoxy than the mechanistic one of seventeenth-century science. And it is on the stage of this clockwork music box that Barth's human characters perform, for whom 'creation is finished and preparatory; nature is impersonal and inert'.[58] But how does this human-centred vision fare when brought into conversation with the more holistic view currently emerging, of a fundamentally integrated cosmos and even a continuing creation? One could argue that it is an example of human sin and egotistical self-absorption to read the history of our vast cosmos as a history of human salvation on one tiny planet at the edge of an indifferent galaxy. And on the Earth itself, to see the eternal fate of human individuals as the only consideration. The creation theologians make both points, calling for a more ecological view of God's interests and commitments, and recognizing that human salvation is as much a matter of living in right relationship with the good Earth than of escaping that Earth to be reconciled with a God set over against creation.[59] On their side is a reasonable reading of Scripture, which while humanly composed, and selected around human interests, nevertheless is peppered with evidence of divine concern for the created order and the other creatures who share our world. Just as women and the poor have opened our eyes to much previously unrecognized teaching about oppression and its cure in Scripture and tradition, through feminist and liberation theologies, so animal rights advocates in theology, such as Andrew Linzey, are drawing our attention in similar ways to the case that can be made for God's interests extending well beyond the human.[60] In Aquinas' universe all the different creatures mattered, composing together a great chain of being fitting in its comprehensiveness to be the work of an unsurpassable creator. Even this pre-modern image is more holistic and ecological than Barth's.

With Barth, as with the liberals previously discussed, there arises the question of *how* God is at work in the world – of seeking to understand this, rather than being content to assert it. In the days of Barth's reformed forebear Schleiermacher there was no evolutionary view in place that had to be taken into account, and in the days of Calvin, whose vision of divine action Barth recovers, there was no self-contained mechanistic explanation of planetary orbits to take into account. The notion of the world as a place of scientific laws which theology must take seriously is something Calvin did not face; nor, fully, did Schleiermacher in his pre-Darwinian era. But can Barth discount it, a contemporary of Einstein and educated in the era when

Darwin's theory swept all before it? Because creation looks very different if it means long evolution, exploitation of chance, advance in the face of chronic randomness through statistical probability, and the emergence of human beings from the natural world through evolution. This and the sheer age of the Earth, the vastness of the cosmos and the extraordinary fine-tuning of physical systems that we now know is necessary for our being here.

For Barth, such wonders as science discloses are meagre representations of God's actual providential care for the cosmos, but to dwell on this and think about the metaphysics of God's action is an inappropriate Christian meditation. But who was it that said 'metaphysics buries its detractors'? Barth is the biblical champion, but he seems unable to express the central biblical conviction that the world is God's good creation, and that human beings are part of that world body and soul. And today science has a far better grasp of the working of that world than Barth admits. Yet Barth leaves the one world of God's one creation bifurcated. He does not seek to understand creation in terms of the world as it is scientifically grasped. But this is not the case even in the Genesis creation accounts, which describe Yahweh's action in terms of the cosmology of the day, over elements of which Yahweh is step by step declared to be Lord – moon and stars, seas, mountains, living things. 'If the same world is the subject of scientific regularities and of providential action,' Barbour inquires of Barth, 'do we not have to show how natural and divine causality can be conceived to coexist?'[61]

The same criticism also applies to Bultmann, though more so. Bultmann cannot meaningfully speak of an act of God in the world, except to say that we believe in them by faith. Bultmann's miracles are Kantian ones, taking place in the changed perspectives that accompany faith. Brian Hebblethwaite tells us that 'when a friend of [his] went to see Bultmann in Marburg some years ago, and asked him to give an example of an act of God, Bultmann replied "a sermon".'[62] Bultmann would have no time for faithless physicists and biologists pontificating about God. But a laudable emphasis on God-talk being self-involving talk rather than idle speculation does not rule out theological reflection on the way God deals with our one world. It is this organic, one world conception that Bultmann's rather Newtonian view of scientific regularities fails to plumb. And with it is his failure to appreciate that humans and their minds are part of the world. But if alcohol, aspirin and adrenaline can make me change my mind, then my mind is not as far from the material world as Bultmann obviously thinks. The world holistically conceived invades Bultmann's Kantian sanctuary of the mind, and possibly vice versa.

With this recognition of human embeddedness in the world arise concerns about the religious risk of such a dualistic programme. In Chapter 2, we saw how downplaying the physical world in favour of God's action led to a reassertion of the physical world's rights in a confident, Godless materialism. And so it is today. Barth's high monotheism, his zeal to deny the deep religious impulse that senses God in nature and his refusal to think of God in relation to scientific reality leave little to anchor faith in an objective God. As a result, 'death of God' theology in the 1960s could reconceive God as an idea only, and question the objective existence of God. Indeed, Bultmann has been queried as to why he did not go further;[63] he has been challenged to take his demythologizing programme to its logical conclusion, demythologizing God and dehistoricizing Christ into images helpful for achieving authentic existence, though of course not essential for it. Here is another instance of God being sought in the self, with a denial of God's objective reality resulting. This is a process we see beautifully laid out for us if we follow the career of the radical English theologian Don Cupitt.[64]

We must now see how God's action might look if today's cosmology and biology are taken with real theological seriousness. In tandem with that, we must face with equal seriousness the issue of tragedy, waste and suffering, the so-called problem of evil. These tasks will occupy us in the next two chapters.

Notes

1 Genesis 1.20–28.

2 Genesis 37; 39–50.

3 Exodus 7–11.

4 Exodus 14–15.

5 Joshua 1–12.

6 Martin Luther, 'Sermon for the First Sunday of Lent', in *Sermons of Martin Luther* (Grand Rapids, MO: Baker, 1988), 2: 141, cited in William C. Placher, *The Domestication of Transcendence: How Modern Thinking about God Went Wrong* (Louisville, KY: Westminster John Knox, 1996), p. 118, n. 35.

7 Isaiah 44.21–45.7.

8 2 Kings 17.5–18; 24.18–25.21.

9 Placher, *Domestication*, p. 190.

10 For Elijah, see 1 Kings 17–19; for David, see 1 and 2 Samuel.

11 Placher, *Domestication*, p. 192.

12 Psalm 104.27–30 (NRSV).

13 See, e.g. 1 Kings 18.17–40; 2 Kings 17.15–18; Ezra 10.11–12.

14 See, e.g. Matthew 8.23–27 and parallels, in which Jesus calms a storm.

15 Owen C. Thomas (ed.), 'Summary analysis', in *God's Activity in the World: The Contemporary Problem* (American Academy of Religion: Studies in Religion 31; Chico, CA: Scholars Press, 1983), pp. 231–40, p. 238.

16 1 Corinthians 15.10 (NRSV).

17 D. M. Baillie, *God Was in Christ: An Essay on Incarnation and Atonement* (1948, 2nd edn 1956) (London: Faber & Faber, 1961), p. 114.

18 Frans Josef van Beeck SJ, *God Encountered: A Contemporary Catholic Systematic Theology*, Vol. 2, Intro. and Pt 1 (Collegeville, MN: Michael Glazier, 1993), p. 289.

19 *Ibid.*, p. 290.

20 'Introduction', in Thomas (ed.) *God's Activity*, pp. 1–14, p. 1 (emphasis mine).

21 See, e.g., Edward Schillebeeckx writing of his Dominican forebear with great affection in 'A saint: Albert the Great', in *God Among Us: The Gospel Proclaimed* (1982) (London: SCM, 1983), pp. 225–31.

22 Placher, *Domestication*, p. 113.

23 Thomas, 'Introduction', p. 2.

24 *Ibid.*; see *Summa theologiae*, Ia, 105, 5 and 2; *Summa contra gentiles*, III, 70.

25 A. D. Sertillanges, *Foundations of Thomistic Philosophy* (Springfield, Ill: Templegate, 1931), p. 154, cited in Ian Barbour, *Issues in Science and Religion* (1966) (London: SCM, 1968), p. 426.

26 Thomas, 'Summary', see *Summa theologiae* Ia, 105, 6.

27 Etienne Gilson, 'The corporeal world and the efficacy of second causes', in Thomas (ed.), *God's Activity*, pp. 213–30, p. 225, excerpted from Gilson, *The Christian Philosophy of St Thomas Aquinas* (New York, NY: Random House, 1956).

28 Thomas, 'Summary', p. 2, citing Calvin, *Institutes of the Christian Religion*, I, xvi, 5.

29 Placher, *Domestication*, pp. 123, 124.

30 *Ibid.*, p. 3.

31 Austin Farrer, *Faith and Speculation: An Essay in Philosophical Theology* (1967) (Edinburgh: T. & T. Clark, 1988), p. 139.

32 See the helpful discussion in Barbour, *Issues*, pp. 23–34.

33 Michel Foucault, *The Order of Things: An Archaeology of the Human Sciences* (New York: Random House, 1973), p. 129, cited in Placher, *Domestication*, p. 129.

34 Barbour, *Issues*, p. 42.

35 Edwin A. Burtt, *The Metaphysical Foundations of Modern Science*, rev. edn (New York: Humanities; London: Routledge & Kegan Paul, 1951), p. 239, cited in Barbour, *Issues*, p. 36.

36 But the God of some deists might still intervene in the course of things, though by no means frivolously. As the leading deist John Toland put it, 'The order of nature is not alterd, stopp'd, or forwarded, unless for some weighty Design becoming the Divine Wisdom and Majesty'; see John Toland, *Christianity Not Mysterious* (London, 1696), cited in Placher, *Domestication*, p. 137, n. 41.

37 Placher, *Domestication*, pp. 136–7.

38 *Ibid.*, p. 138.

39 David Hume, *Enquiry Concerning Human Understanding* (1748), Section 10, 'Of miracles', excerpted in Richard Swinburne (ed.), *Miracles* (New York: Macmillan, 1989), pp. 23–40, p. 29.

40 Placher, *Domestication*, p. 135.

41 *Ibid.*, p. 145.

42 Barbour, *Issues*, p. 67.

43 William Wordsworth, 'Tintern Abbey' (1798).

44 Thomas, 'Introduction', p. 4.

45 Helpful here is the discussion by Thomas F. Tracy, 'Particular providence and the God of the gaps', in Robert John Russell, Nancey Murphy and Arthur R. Peacocke (eds), *Chaos and Complexity: Scientific Perspectives on Divine Action* (2nd edn) (Vatican City State: Vatican Observatory; Berkeley, CA: Center for Theology and the Natural Sciences, 1997), pp. 289–324, pp. 295–301.

46 *Ibid.*, p. 298.

47 F. D. E. Schleiermacher, *On Religion: Speeches to its Cultured Despisers* (New York: Harper & Row, 1958), p. 88, cited in Thomas, 'Summary', p. 298.

48 Maurice Wiles, *God's Action in the World* (London: SCM, 1986), p. 29.

49 John Hick, 'Prayer, providence and miracle', in John Hick and Michael Goulder, *Why Believe in God?* (London: SCM, 1983), pp. 64–80; see also John Hick (ed.), *The Myth of God Incarnate* (London: SCM, 1977).

50 Barbour, *Issues*, p. 112.

51 Gordon D. Kaufman, 'On the meaning of "Act of God"', *Harvard Theological Review*, **61** (1968), pp. 175–201.

52 G. Ernest Wright, *God Who Acts: Biblical Theology as Recital* (London: SCM, 1952).

53 Langdon Gilkey, 'Cosmology, ontology and the travail of biblical language', *The Journal of Religion*, **41** (1961), pp. 194–205.

54 Karl Barth, *Church Dogmatics*, III, 3 (Edinburgh: T. & T. Clark, 1960), p. 129.

55 *Ibid.*

56 Rudolf Bultmann, 'Bultmann replies to his critics', in Hans Werner Bartsch (ed.), *Kerygma and Myth: A Theological Debate* (1953) (London: SPCK, 1954), pp. 191–211, p. 197.

57 Rudolf Bultmann, *Jesus Christ and Mythology* (New York: Charles Scribner's Sons, 1958), p. 68.

58 Barbour, *Issues*, p. 424.

59 See, e.g. Matthew Fox, *The Coming of the Cosmic Christ: The Healing of Mother Earth and the Birth of a Global Renaissance* (1988)(Melbourne: Collins-Dove, 1989).

60 See Andrew Linzey, *Animal Theology* (London: SCM, 1994), and his intriguing *Animal Rites: Liturgies of Animal Care* (London: SCM, 1999); also Andrew Linzey and Tom Regan (eds), *Animals and Christianity: A Book of Readings* (London: SPCK, 1988); Andrew Linzey and Dorothy Yamamoto (eds), *Animals on the Agenda: Questions About Animals for Theology and Ethics* (London: SCM, 1998).

61 Barbour, *Issues*, p. 425.
62 Brian Hebblethwaite, 'Providence and divine action', *Religious Studies*, **14** (1978), pp. 223–36, p. 225.
63 See, e.g. Schubert Ogden, *Christ Without Myth* (New York: Harper & Row, 1961).
64 Cupitt begins with a high monotheism in the 1960s and by the 1980s is reducing God to an image of possible utility in shaping the self: see my *Atheist Priest? Don Cupitt and Christianity* (London: SCM, 1988).

5 Divine Action: Scientific Questions

It is the burden of our tale that the scientifically discerned process of the world is sufficiently flexible to permit both God and us to work within it.

John Polkinghorne, *Science and Providence*, 1989

We have so far concluded that to imagine God in today's cultural context is a matter of reminting our God-images, because a God remote from the world and from experience is a God who slips from belief. This we saw happening in the eighteenth century, following the misbegotten efforts of seventeenth-century theology in its eager removal of God from the newly closed world of mechanistic science. Thus God became superfluous, because life could increasingly be lived without reference to God in the bustling bourgeois world of technology and market forces then coming to birth, because God seemed unnecessary to explain a universe which science was successfully unfolding, because the God of Bible and Church tradition active in the world was left with less and less of a stage on which to perform – with increasingly fewer gaps in the tightening straitjacket of natural causality. At the same time the problem of evil and suffering in a world growing used to intricate design and efficiency began to make belief in an omnipotent, omnibenevolent creator and sustainer increasingly problematic.

In this chapter I am going to introduce the idea that none of this is fatal for belief in a God who acts in the world. William Pollard, an American priest and physicist, no doubt accurately read the signs a generation ago when he wrote 'It is a most difficult thing for the scientifically trained mind to conceive how God could act in His world.'[1] But today in mainstream Christian literature a priest and physicist like John Polkinghorne, along with a priest and biochemist like Arthur Peacocke, can present a world sufficiently open that divine action need no longer seem as problematic as once it did, when a constricting definition of scientific law dominated.

God in an open universe

We now consider some options that have been advanced in conversation between theology and late twentieth-century science for reconceiving divine action. One option softens the rigidity of scientific law, another explores the possibility of quantum effects and their amplification being the way God acts. The realm of chaotic dynamics is also considered as a possible area in which God might work, and the way in which whole systems influence their parts. We also briefly note an openness to paranormal factors which is entertained by some in theology today.

Softening scientific law

One way toward theorizing divine action in a post-Newtonian world is to question the completeness of scientific laws. In the last chapter we saw this approach taken by Barth, with a Kantian account of scientific law understood to be imposed by human minds on the actual workings of God, which transcend human understanding and always will. From this perspective one could easily assert a double agency view, or even the occasionalism of Malebranche, according to which God does everything and the created world is an insubstantial veil over the real driving force of reality, which is God. But since Thomas Aquinas few have sensed any glory for God accruing in such diminishment of God's creation.[2]

Without disregarding natural laws, in the manner of Barth, one can simply see these laws as only a limited approximation to nature. It is a major strategy in contemporary discussion to offer such a weak realist account of scientific laws, leaving enough room for divine action alongside them. Instead of God working behind a veil of nature, as in Barth, this view takes nature more seriously, with God working through it rather than behind it. It is a weak realist view in that scientific theory is only an approximation to nature, an incomplete account. Nevertheless, nature and our own grasp of its laws are taken more seriously here than we have seen to be the case with Barth.

Austin Farrer, a leading Anglo-Catholic thinker of the last generation, whose mature views on divine action are a major starting point for contemporary discussions, provides one version of this approach. He questions whether a universe exists at all, with its own objective laws, while taking seriously the behaviour of particular creatures, insisting that 'general laws are not the real forces which compose the universe, any more than the Queen's Regulations are the Army and Navy.'[3] Jesuit priest and astrophysicist William Stoeger holds another weak realist view, for whom God works through the laws that are actually there, rather than our limited approximations of them, by which we describe but will never explain nature.[4] John Polkinghorne takes the same approach, though unlike Stoeger he looks forward to the day when physics will be unified and simplified with a new overarching theory, against which divine action will be more readily conceivable. For Polkinghorne, today's physics represents 'asymptotically emergent-downward approximations to that greater truth'.[5]

But in advance of a fuller physics, able to slot together more readily with theology (whether or not such a vision splendid will be granted this side of the eschaton), we must ask whether there is enough to be going on with in our present physics, so that in dialogue with theology divine action might again seem to be at home in the world, as was the pre-modern situation, rather than the imposition upon the world which divine action has regularly seemed since the seventeenth century. The theory of divine action we seek, as Philip Clayton sets it out,

> Requires an open world, one with causal spaces in which God could act. Moreover, these must be such that natural law is not suspended or broken every time God acts, which would make a mockery of the natural order. Finally, it must be the sort of openness that will not be closed up by advances in scientific knowledge, leaving theologians stranded high and dry (again). The history of embarrassment is long enough already.[6]

And this is the sort of thing which our present physics offers, though there is still plenty of debate over the details.

Divine action and quantum physics?

The question has to do with how God might be at work in a universe of regular scientific laws, in which it is plainly the case that God's actions are not plain – that if God is at work, then it is 'in, with and under' the world process, rather than observably within it. Where are the gaps, and not just gaps in our present understanding? Where are the gaps in the *ontology*, not only in the *epistemology*? There are various answers.

The first major attempt at thinking this way was by William Pollard, the aforementioned Episcopal priest and physicist, who took the realm of quantum indeterminacy for the necessary ontological gap. He believed that God directed quantum events toward one or another outcome, and so providentially guided events in the world, acting within the (in principle) forever unknowable realm of the Heisenberg Uncertainty Principle. When by experiment and observation we can know only statistical probabilities, at the quantum level, and maybe at other levels of the system forever beyond examination, nevertheless God could be at work. And sometimes only small changes would be needed to shift a major historical outcome, as in the bad weather that wrecked the Spanish Armada, or helped Washington defeat Cornwallis at Yorktown. As one American historian wrote, quoted approvingly by Pollard, 'the turning points are made of such stuff as this: of a shifting wind and a courtier's shyness, of a woman's greed and an old man's hatred, of a metal's failure and a soldier's blunder.'[7] According to Pollard, this is the way God guides events, through tiny nudges at the quantum level forever hidden from our sight.

A most thorough and significant recent development of Pollard's case is offered by Nancey Murphy. She follows Barth in deontologizing the laws of nature, and interprets God as supplying the bits of activity that our present physical account of the world cannot provide. In short, her God is the hidden variable which Einstein had sought in vain against the Copenhagen School, with its probabilistic reading of quantum theory. Quantum-level outcomes, like determining the location of an electron, or through which of two diffraction slits a photon passes, or whether a radioisotope decays, are matters of probability. Which outcome will be realized, and why, is unknown, apart from statistical probabilities in aggregate outcomes from enormous numbers of such processes. For Murphy, however, there is no such randomness. It is God who chooses, who collapses the wave function of probabilities leaving only the single measured outcome. Yet this divine act is not an interruption of the natural order, according to Murphy, for whom 'there is no competition between God and nature because, *ex hypothesi*, the efficient natural causes at this level are insufficient to determine all the outcomes.'[8] Murphy is aware of alternative accounts by which God might influence physical reality, and to these we will soon be referring, but she is confident that such other ways God might be at work in natural systems must eventually boil down to her account – of particular atomic events being determined by God, albeit within the closed weave of apparent probabilistic outcomes and quantum indeterminacy.

An important consideration here has to do with the sort of gaps needed if God's work is to proceed without rupturing fundamental nature. Is this really an ontological gap, a 'proper gap', this realm of the collapsing wave function, or just an epistemological one? In other words, what if a competing hidden variable explanation were found? Would Murphy's God then disappear into the gap she has prepared? Does not the shade of Laplace arise at this point, and his dismissal of the necessary divine intervention Newton required to make his physics of planetary motion work out? While it is important for Murphy that this is an ontological gap, that whatever collapses the wave function of probabilities will never be known by physics, the history of physics makes it difficult to share her confidence.

Small-scale influence, large-scale effect?

While it is one thing to make an electron present itself here or there for measurement, it is another to make changes in the macroscopic world. And here there is some controversy. One can imagine single quantum events that change things in the world we see, such as the one uranium isotope decaying which starts a chain reaction which makes the atomic bomb go off, or the influences at molecular level that may trigger genetic mutations with results for a whole organism[9] and, if advantageous, for the future evolution of species. And there is the emerging area of quantum technology, where manipulation of events at the quantum level is employed in working toward new technologies, in electronics and communications. In particular there is so-called 'quantum computing', which seeks to use quantum phenomena in real-world computational tasks, with enormous time savings in view.[10]

But a lot of quantum events in the normal run of things will be balanced out, without making their mark at the level of macroscopic change. For this reason, David Bartholomew argues that for God to achieve a desired outcome it would be sufficient for God to leave the great majority of events to chance and work only in the events where a particular outcome is desired. He also points out that chance processes can lead to more or less determinate ends. Insurance companies depend on the unpredictable outcomes of millions of lives yielding a regular enough death rate that competitive premiums can be set. In the same way, chance and randomness stimulate creation to explore options toward the fuller evolution of life, and to bounce back from upset or disruption. This is also the case in games which involve a mixture of chance and skill, where if skill lets you down the throw of dice or the turn of a card may provide a fresh way forward. It could be imagined that a wise creator would make just such a resilient world, which would not need to be constantly guided micro-event by micro-event, as Pollard and Murphy would have it.[11] Chance and law are a powerful combination that allow things to develop in games, and in nature, too, as far as we know, which appears to be the realm of both the novel and the reliable, the random and the determined.

Another problem for the close manipulation of numerous events as a model for divine action is the number of steps along a causal chain that are involved, the many causal chains which must coincide for a particular outcome to be achieved and the interference caused by competing causal chains working toward other outcomes at the same time. As David Bartholomew puts it, with dizzying effect,

> the production of a particular 'accident' may require the manipulation of a large number of roots and it is not clear that this number can be kept sufficiently small to avoid causing a more serious problem. In proceeding toward an 'accident' the contributory causal chains will intersect with many others all proceeding on their way to other intended accidents. At any one time there will then be a multitude of inter-weaving and inter-acting sequences sparking off accidents as they intersect. All of these accidents either have to have been 'designed' or foreseen to be harmless or, at least, tolerable. The complexity of the situation defies imagination. It is many orders of magnitude more complex than a game of chess in which not only must the end be foreseen, but also every other event along the way. In view of all this it is far from clear that history can be adequately controlled by manipulation of happenings at the roots.[12]

Involved in this is a question about whether quantum events are regularly able to blow up to macroscopic scale, except perhaps in a few instances like those mentioned above. This so-called 'measurement problem' impinges on the question of divine action, but the answer is not agreed. Bartholomew says 'not necessarily', as we have seen, and Polkinghorne is not sanguine about the links some establish between quantum events and the macroscopic world via the amplifying effect of chaos theory.[13] The aspect of chaos theory referred to here is the extraordinary sensitivity to initial conditions exhibited by many macroscopic systems, like the weather, or the amplification of feedback, or heart arrhythmia, or a marble balancing on the top of a wire – which way will it fall? All these natural systems are critically influenced by tiny changes, to many decimal places of apparent insignificance. The question is, does this so-called 'butterfly effect' extend so far down that quantum phenomena can be regularly amplified via such means to influence outcomes in the world we can see? While some say 'no', others say 'yes', or at least 'maybe', which is the case for theologian Thomas Tracy,[14] while physicist George Ellis[15] is more confident. Tracy is content with the possibility of some quantum level acts of God that can be amplified, leaving the majority of quantum events to chance, seeking to steer a middle course between Pollard and Bartholomew.

Divine influence at higher levels?

Leaving the discussion of quantum events for now, we consider the possibility of other kinds of divine action in natural systems as understood by today's physics. We have noted the possibility that quantum events may be amplified through the sensitivity to initial conditions displayed by dynamic systems as described in chaos theory. But this same realm provides another type of irreducible 'gap' in which God might work, just as quantum systems do. Chaos theory is a deterministic theory, finding deep order in the way apparently chaotic behaviour in natural systems conceals stable states known as 'strange attractors', toward which the system is drawn. But the theory also recognizes some zones of apparent chaos and randomness in the behaviour of dynamic systems which no known mathematical test can declare to be determinate, and non-random. Consequently, if God were to do something to influence such a dynamic system in such a regime, we would never know. As Wildman and Russell point out, 'Chaos theory might have made the case for metaphysical determinism stronger than it has ever been before, but chaos theory also guarantees that the case cannot get any stronger.'[16] So here is another 'gap' in which God might be at work, though is it just one more gap in knowledge rather than an ontological gap? And gaps in knowledge do have a habit of being closed, as the history of physics abundantly teaches.

Related to this, as against the 'bottom-up' causality we have been considering, is the notion of 'top-down' causality. Instead of influencing the whole beginning with a part, this is about affecting the parts by an influence on the whole. There are many examples. Lower the temperature of a conducting wire close to absolute zero and its electrical resistance disappears, so the electric current will flow without diminishment if the power is switched off. In this phenomenon, known as superconductivity, sufficiently cooling the metal eventually induces its electrons to form 'Cooper pairs' which move more readily through the metal. The functioning of lasers, by which stimulation of a gas or a crystal causes molecules to resonate in a particular way, provides another example. The system influences its parts to act differently from how they act in isolation. Convection is another instance, in which molecules of fluid in a heated cell or of air above a desert floor move uniformly in a regular rolling pattern, entering regimes of turbulence and of deterministic chaos. Arthur Peacocke points to the way evolutionary selection can be said to change DNA, and to conscious states of the brain as a whole influencing particular neurones, and hence bodily actions.

Whether it is 'top-down' or, more correctly, 'whole-part', the idea is that the state of the whole or of the more complex entity acts as a cause or a constraint upon the part, with the science appropriate at the higher level unable to be explicated in terms of what science at the lower level would expect. This is the phenomenon of 'emergent complexity' at work, in which aggregates and systems demonstrate behaviours and complexities different from how their parts would behave alone. Crystals have a different behaviour from that evident in their constituent molecules taken alone. Electrons behave differently depending on whether they are in a semiconductor or in a metal, and if a metal whether they are at the surface (fewer neighbours) or in the bulk (more neighbours). Phase changes (steam to liquid to ice) bring out different behaviours in the water molecules involved. My cat is different now that his former companions are no longer with us, influencing his behaviour (he has ceased to be defensively voracious at mealtimes, for instance). Flocks of birds, schools of fish and herds of antelope exhibit dramatic synchronous turning behaviour that is not evident when you view them in isolation. And a lump of greyish meat involving sufficient complex connectedness of neurones becomes the carrier of human consciousness. Peacocke argues that this is the way God can be seen to be at work in the world, influencing wholes and thereby changing things at the level of parts. Peacocke's God works 'primarily on the world-as-a-whole, but thereby on any constituent entity or event in the world that God wishes to influence in a top-down manner through the boundary conditions and constraints that the state of the whole exerts upon all subsidiary, constituent entities and processes'.[17]

For Peacocke it is inappropriate to search 'bottom-up' for God at work among quantum phenomena in the way we have been considering 'for it does not do justice to the many levels in which causality operates in a world of complex systems multiply interlocking at many levels and in many modes.'[18] John Polkinghorne agrees, declaring distasteful this ascription to God of a 'hole-in-the-corner way of influencing quantum events'.[19] Polkinghorne does point out, however, that a lot of so-called 'top-down' effects can be understood as influences between parts, rather than entirely of the whole upon the part. So, for instance, the sensitivity to initial conditions of chaotic systems not only reflects the effect of the whole environment on the piece in question, but is also about all the parts of that environment each having their influence. In the same way, while the freezing of water is about the effect of environment on the water molecules taken as a whole, we must also take into account the complex patterns of freezing that are generated from one part to another in the fluid, as is comparably the case with all forms of crystal growth.[20] Polkinghorne prefers to look at 'top-down' and 'bottom-up' processes together for an adequate account of natural phenomena and, by extension, divine action. Actually, so does Peacocke, who affirms that both are necessary, while insisting that the more holistic 'whole-part' approach needs to be emphasized against the systemic reductionism characteristic of science since the Enlightenment.[21]

Polkinghorne seeks to clarify his own suggestion by declaring God's actions to be through the conveying of information, rather than the expending of energy. Such vanishingly tiny perturbations are able to shift a chaotic system while to all intents and purposes the changes happen without the energy of the system changing. The system follows whichever of 'the many different trajectories through the attractor's phase space (that is, the range of its future possible states) which all correspond to the same energy'[22] in response not to energetic nudges by God, but by what Polkinghorne calls 'information'. And here we suspect the fuller physics toward which he looks is being invoked in the present.

Paranormal phenomena

I mention one last possibility, rather different from the previous ones. We noted in the last chapter how the fuller, Aristotelian conception of four causes was much reduced in the seventeenth century, so that since Descartes 'efficient causality' was the only cause that really mattered. This is certainly the case with options canvassed in the preceding discussion. It is a search for causal chains, and when the talk is of whole influencing part the language is vaguest. And this because the science is vaguest. We know about efficient causality, but any other sort is less obvious to the modern scientific temper of mind.

In this connection it is important to mention the paranormal. Mainstream science does not take this option seriously, but there are notable individual exceptions to this rule. C. G. Jung introduced the term 'synchronicity' to cover a range of phenomena he regularly encountered himself and among his patients. He mentions runs of coincidences that seem meaningful, extraordinary stories of things that come back to their owners, precognition in dreams, birds drawn to houses at the time of their occupants' deaths, and one particular event which made quite an impression on him: while a patient was recounting a dream about a golden scarab, an insect very like one began flying at the window, unaccountably trying to enter Jung's darkened consulting room. Unconscious images coming to consciousness in correlation with objective happenings is the gist of this synchronicity, which Jung understands to be an acausal principle of explanation. He writes, 'our conception of causality is incapable of explaining the facts.'[23]

Keith Ward is one mainstream theologian willing to define miracle in terms of the paranormal.[24] Others suggest that intercessory prayer may work naturally for the good of its objects through telepathy,[25] exploiting hitherto unexplained natural connections at a distance between human beings that could serve as carriers of compassion. A world full of dynamic systems sensitive to inconceivably minute influences in their initial conditions is just the sort of world in which such things might happen. It may be sufficient in such situations to sense a fuller account of the natural, beckoning us to take so-called paranormal phenomena more seriously.

This possibility of telepathy and 'synchronicity' would also be in keeping with the new openness to a weakly realist account of scientific law found in theology today. Can we admit that nature is richer and more complex than our mathematical models of nature indicate, beyond a rigid scientism which refuses even to consider the type of cases Jung brings before us? Chaos theory has reminded us of this over recent decades, changing long-held convictions with a whole new appreciation of the complexity of things once thought simple, along with a new appreciation of deep order in processes once consigned to randomness.

Reconceiving divine action: three roads not taken

What I have tried to do in this chapter so far is to provide a clean scientific page. But it is as yet unclear what are the most appropriate theological conclusions to write upon it. In the next chapter I want to present a version of the double agency paradox of Christian antiquity, including the possibility of special and not just uniform divine action, as a conceivable answer for today. But first we ought to set aside three current alternatives that I believe to be less helpful. There is the option of complete divine determination of every event. There is process theology, which sees God as a lure, contributing to the outcome of every event. And then there is the radical recent suggestion of Ruth Page that God is best thought of as companion and pain bearer to the world, but not as its creator, and not as acting within it. We might call these three options 'God does everything', 'God lures everything' and 'God loves everything', respectively.

God does everything?

The idea that God directly causes all events in the universe while nature is a shadowy non-contributor is something we met in the 'occasionalism' of Malebranche in Chapter 2, above. We saw something very like it in Karl

Barth, too, in our Chapter 4 discussion of his views. This approach re-emerges in our dialogue with scientific options in the work of Pollard and Murphy, whose conclusions about God and quantum indeterminacy we have noted.

For Murphy, all the myriad quantum events that comprise every tiny corner of an incomprehensibly vast universe 'require God's cooperation in order to be actualised'.[26] Nature at this basic level, below the reach of our sight, is God at work, though at the macroscopic level all normally expected regularities are maintained, and nature does its own thing. But does this God really let nature go its own way, in tandem with God's own acts, or does God really do everything? Might it rather be that genuine randomness is in the nature of these quantum events – in the spirit of Aquinas, might we see genuine randomness as something God respects in nature and uses,[27] so that the removal of genuine randomness from quantum phenomena would not be God's way, as Murphy suggests it is? The diminishment of the creation is a key theological issue here, which as we have noted is anathema to the mainstream double agency tradition. We have seen that a world scolded and derided by theology in the seventeenth century struck back in the powerful case its regularities gave to atheistic scientific reductionism.

Let us dwell on some implications of this fundamental determinism for a moment. Does it not follow that a world fully determined at the fundamental level is a world of illusion, a world where randomness is an illusion, and all freedom with it, both natural and human? Is it not then a Truman Burbank world, only more so, because the control extends into the subjectivity of every acting person? Worse than a world like that portrayed in *The Truman Show*, then, it evokes the vertiginous world of systematic deception portrayed in another nervous late nineties, pre-millennial movie, *The Matrix*. There human life is an inert, unconscious terror masked by a credible computer-generated reality suffusing human consciousness via a brain implant. To take another metaphor, such a world is like a puppet show. The puppet is meant to evoke a person, but is clearly not the real thing. The puppet has someone's hand up it. And so it is with a fully determined universe, 'worked' by God at the quantum level, or within chaotic regimes, or by whatever other means a whole cosmos might be fully controlled, 'top-down' if not 'bottom-up'. This is a world rather like a puppet, resembling the real thing but not the real thing. But it is a rather more sinister world than the charming world of puppets.

Our unease here is linked to another key theological issue, and that is the way this fully determined view of things conflicts with what we believe about God's action in Christ and in our own lives. Double agency is something Christians experience, with Christ as the limiting case, according to an argument offered at the beginning of Chapter 4. Freedom to act and yet the conviction that God is fully expressed in certain acts is something Christians believe about their own lives and about Christ, who incarnated God in the choices of an acting person and the life these choices shaped. Genuine human freedom is as important here as the divine activity, and without the former the latter is shown to be of a different character than expected, not personal nor gracious nor the manifestation of a relationship, but oddly impersonal, formulaic and mechanical. Can we really accept that God is doing everything in our lives, though unlike Calvin and earlier advocates of predestination there is no sense in which we are doing it too? The whole notion of covenant is incompatible with this, as is our self-understanding as free agents. Both revealed and natural theology must take issue with such a view.

God lures everything?

Process theology is based on the idea that God forms *part of* the cause of each and every event. Following Whitehead it takes a fully relational view of reality – each entity is influenced by each other entity, 'prehended' by it. And God, like the highest monad of Leibniz, is prehended by all and prehends all. God is thus in creative, influencing relationship with all of reality, but also experiences all of reality. The process God grounds a world in which change and novelty are essential dimensions of its order; process thinking successfully disposes of God as the ground of a statically conceived cosmos.

So far so good? It is important to note that the process view diverges from the tradition's commitment to double agency. Process theologians John Cobb and David Ray Griffin declare double agency to be unintelligible, as well as untenable in light of the fact of evil.[28] They are not exactly searching for a mechanism of divine action, for a 'causal joint'[29] between God and the cosmos, but they are seeking an intelligible account of how it is that God can be at work when nature and humanity are at work, in the same actions. The process solution is that God is the lure in every event toward actualizing the 'initial aim' that God has given that event, but it is up to the event itself to go along. This God, who persuades but does not control, is a God of love primarily and not power. This God, according to the Anglican process theologian Norman Pittenger, (1) sets up a ground plan for the future evolution of the cosmos, (2) initiates novelty in the emergence of complexity, then life and eventually consciousness, (3) lures every event and every creature to grasp its possibilities toward realizing its optimum goal, then (4) 'God receives into his own existence whatever has been actualised, sifting out the good from the deviant or distorted', whereupon (5) 'God harmonises in his own life that which has been contributed to him.'[30] Thus in God's 'consequent nature' God takes up all that is good in the cosmos, redeeming it and somehow redeploying that redeemed reality in the world.

Having heard double agency criticized for unintelligibility, however, with its talk of God working in and through secondary causes, this process account is not self-evidently more intelligible. Its great strength is that it represents the first serious attempt to think divine action in an evolutionary view of the world. But the devil is in the detail.

I question the appropriateness of 'lure' as an exhaustive way of explaining human motivation, not to mention the behaviour of non-conscious agents. Humans know what it means to be 'lured' toward the optimum realization of their inbuilt potential. We know the seductive craft of the good teacher deftly drawing the best from students, or the inspiration of seeing a fine musician play which drives us to practise, or the sense of our own best self that the integrity, the transparent goodness of others can inspire in us. But just as often we are driven compulsively, not lured – we are forced to the gym by our restless endorphins (not all of us, however), or carried away by our sexual impulses; we find ourselves unable to resist the favourite addictive 'hit', from narcotics to shopping to potato crisps; humans are regularly consumed with anger, or overwhelmed by compassion, and in such cases there is little experience of choosing. This is the other side of concerns expressed in the previous discussion, of reality being fully determined. There, the fact of human choice and freedom had to be given credence; here, it is the fact of human compulsion. For every experience of being lured, we can point to one in which our action seems determined – the drink did it, the gonads did it, the energy of the moment did it, carrying us along. All of these instances point to primary causes working through secondary causes – the desire working through the means by which we fulfil it. So claims that process thought is truer to our experience than double agency merit examination.

In the same way, we must ask what 'lure' might mean for a proton, for a projectile, for a pumpkin. One can imagine an animal being 'lured' – herein lies the fisher's art and the cat fancier's perennial challenge. But the 'panpsychism' of those who account for consciousness at higher levels by positing sparks of it at lower, subanimate levels, and who go on to propose some sort of divine exchange in every instance of matter doing its thing, are not significantly advancing the clarity of explanation beyond the traditional doctrine of double agency. The difference, in terms of substance in the argument, seems to be between God acting and God influencing acts, with the detail no more profoundly plumbed in the process case than in the double agency one. John Polkinghorne thinks process talk needs to be fleshed out in terms of actual physics, apart from which it is too vague. He writes, 'God's interaction is not energetic but informational. I believe my account is a kind of demythologisation of what is unclearly articulated by those who use words like "lure" or "influence" or "guidance".'[31]

Another matter, before we leave the process option. And that is the gap between the robust God of the Bible, who wades into human history to save and to judge, to heal and to destroy, and the more gentle, patient God of process thinking, Whitehead's 'fellow-sufferer who understands'. Keith Ward, for one, is convinced that neither a serious view of evil nor faith in a liberating God is adequately served by process thinking. He asks,

Is it appropriate for God merely to endure and persuade when his creatures are being tortured and destroyed? Perhaps the more he seeks to persuade, the more he will be treated with contempt, as a god without power or sanction for his will. Whitehead's view requires a very long perspective, in which creatures may eventually tire of self and, out of sheer exhaustion of desire, turn back to God. But what of those who suffer oppression now? And what of those who may not tire of evil, who revel in the destruction they cause?

The same criticism, though even more pointed, applies to the next option we consider.

God loves everything?

Ruth Page, of the Edinburgh Divinity faculty, sees God as a great lover, but not a God at work in the world nor even the creator of that world. Page writes theology from a committed environmental perspective. In her intriguing study *God and the Web of Creation* she investigates the issue of divine action in the world with an eye to all the complex interrelatedness of the natural order, and with a suspicion of the anthropocentricity characterizing Western tradition, which in Bultmann for instance reduced the realm of reliable divine action to that of pious human interiority. Hers is a savvy, postmodern perspective, attuned to the ideological colouring of theology. So Page recognizes that the standard notion of divine action as controlling events and directing outcomes, as robustly making things happen, reflects masculine conceptions of action, which we in Australia would call 'blokey'. Page prefers a less patriarchally shaped discourse, seeing divine action as the establishment of relationship with the world, rather than God imposing outcomes on the world.[32] Her real motivation is the problem of evil, however, which makes the virile God of providence seem intolerably improvident, answerable for human evil to be sure, but also for extraordinary suffering and waste in the animal realm, including the disappearance of 98 per cent of all species that have ever existed. Against the full-blooded God of making and doing, Page admits that her alternative may seem anaemic, but she believes no other theology can be borne in the face of so much acute animal and human suffering.[33]

And her alternative? It is in effect a sophisticated merger of Gnosticism, maybe deism, perhaps the Eastern Orthodox doctrine of energies, certainly aspects of panentheism, along with the involved, suffering God we meet in theologies of the cross, such as that of Moltmann, all transposed into an environmental key. Page's God does not create the world, but creates possibility, from which the world emerges. Her God is 'with everything', experiencing life from within at all its levels, and suffers with the creation in all its parts, but without making, sustaining or intervening. Panentheism and the relational God-images that go with it, which we considered in Chapter 3, do not take away the problems Page has identified. So she coins a new term, *Pansyntheism*, God-with-everything, God in relation to everything. Her God is like the panentheistic God in that her God 'is *in* the process, *with* the creatures, not *over* or *beyond* the interrelated processes of the world',[34] but God's action is only to seek relationship, to accompany, to watch over.

Here I was reminded of the film *Wings of Desire* by Wim Wenders, and its American spin-off, *City of Angels*, imagining the world full of invisible angels full of delight and compassion in their dealings with humans, straining to be close in joy and sadness, in risk and tragedy, and always alongside the dying, full of pain when their 'good thoughts' come to no effect. Yet their presence is hardly sensed, and they cannot avert disaster. Their *pansyntheism* is moving, but it is not effectual, and at worst might even be seen as voyeuristic. Certainly, it has little in common with the biblical God, not to mention the biblical angels.

To add some effectuality to her view of God, Page offers eschatological comfort, declaring that God will preserve all that is valuable in the world and in individual lives in God's own life eternally. In this we hear echoes of a process approach whereby God's 'consequent nature' is augmented by all that is worthwhile in creation. God maintains relationship with such 'moments of concurrence' at all times, when God's will and that of creatures has come into synchronization.[35] But one wonders again about the biblical God, who hates nothing God has made, who does not lack stomach in the face of contradiction, distortion and sin but meets them head on, redemptively. The biblical God is a saviour whereas Page's God is a filter. Perhaps the many rich sources of a more robust feminine imagery need to be tapped, then, because concrete divine action, which grasps the nettle of history, need not be cursed by patriarchalism. There is certainly an old-fashioned tenor of unflinching manliness in the way English writers like Keith Ward and Austin Farrer write about divine action, whose God like a commanding officer has the stomach to allow suffering for the sake of a greater good, though like any good officer their God is not unmoved. But there is nothing necessarily patriarchal about a God who takes responsibility. More of this in the next chapter.

A limited outcome

Let us now sum up. We have been considering means by which God's action might be thought alongside contemporary accounts of the way things go in nature. What we have found is an openness very different from the closed world of d'Holbach and others since the seventeenth century. There are 'gaps' in the account of nature that may cloak divine action. While some are 'epistemological gaps', that may one day be closed by the advance of science, others might indeed be 'ontological gaps' that would never then be closable, wedged open forever by the Heisenberg Uncertainty Principle, or the impenetrable randomness of chaotic regimes or the ways wholes influence parts. 'There is a sense', concludes John Polkinghorne, 'in which all free action, ours or God's, depends upon "gaps", the inherent incompletenesses which make openness possible.'[36]

In particular, we have been considering options whereby God might actually do all of this, in tentative comments about how God might achieve an end through some quantum effect, chaotic amplification or whole-part influence. Note, however, that this sort of thing is always presented as a possibility in these pages rather than a plain actuality. We must admit that all we have achieved in this chapter in terms of such specifics is *that* God might be able to act through the natural world, rather than to conclude finally just *how* God might act. Austin Farrer points out that we are sure of divine action in the same way that an amateur is sure that the painting in view is a Rembrandt, even though the amateur cannot specify all the technical information about brush strokes and so forth that would absolutely settle it. In the same way Farrer is confident that 'The causal joint . . . between God's action and ours is of no concern in the activities of religion: the very idea of it arises simply as a by-product of the analogical imagination.'[37]

So it has been important to establish that God can act in the world without doing violence to science, and our discussion involved some specific suggestions, though these are not assured solutions. Having established the possibility of thinking divine action in today's open universe, perhaps Philip Clayton is right about how and how not to proceed from there.

> Perhaps it would be better, once the initial possibility of divine action has been won, to leave behind detailed questions of means and mechanisms. Otherwise the danger arises that our theories will sound Aristotelian in the sense that the early modern thinkers derided: making postulations about the nature of events in the physical world for which we have no empirical evidence.[38]

In what follows, therefore, we will assume God's action and reflect on it at the level of theology, without presuming that we have worked out the detailed mechanics of God's action – *that* God can act in our world will suffice for us, as we consider the sort of things God might do, rather than expecting to conclude precisely *how* God might do them.

When this book was at its proof stage, a further volume in a series referred to in this chapter arrived on my desk. Had it been possible, I would have studied and worked with its insights. See Robert John Russell, William R. Stoeger SJ and Francisco J. Ayala (eds), *Evolutionary and Molecular Biology: Scientific Perspectives on Divine Action*. (Vatican City State: Vatican Observatory Publications; Berkeley: Center for Theology and the Natural Sciences, 1998.)

Notes

1 William Pollard, *Chance and Providence* (1958) (London: Faber & Faber, 1959), p. 11.

2 *Summa contra gentiles*, III, 70.

3 Austin Farrer, *Love Almighty and Ills Unlimited* (London: Collins, 1962), p. 97; see also *Faith and Speculation: An Essay in Philosophical Theology* (1967) (Edinburgh: T. & T. Clark, 1988), p. 163.

4 William Stoeger SJ, 'Contemporary physics and the ontological stature of the laws of nature', in Robert John Russell, Nancey Murphy and C. J. Isham (eds), *Quantum Cosmology and the Laws of Nature: Scientific Perspectives on Divine Action* (2nd edn) (Vatican City State: Vatican Observatory Publications; Berkeley, CA: The Center for Theology and the Natural Sciences, 1996), pp. 207–31.

5 John Polkinghorne, 'The laws of nature and the laws of physics', in *Quantum Cosmology*, pp. 429–40, p. 440.

6 Philip D. Clayton, *God and Contemporary Science* (Edinburgh Studies in Constructive Theology; Grand Rapids, MI: Eerdmans, 1997), p. 212.

7 Oscar Handlin, *Chance or Destiny: Turning Points in American History* (Little, Brown & Co, 1955), cited in Pollard, *Chance*, p. 70.

8 Nancey Murphy, 'Divine action in the natural order: Buridan's ass and Schrödinger's cat', in Robert John Russell, Nancey Murphy and Arthur R. Peacocke (eds), *Chaos and Complexity: Scientific Perspectives on Divine Action* (2nd edn) (Vatican City State: Vatican Observatory Publications; Berkeley, CA: The Center for Theology and the Natural Sciences, 1997), pp. 325–57, p. 343.

9 'DNA responds to quantum events, as when mutations are produced by single photons, with consequences that may be macroscopic – leukemia, for example.' I. Percival, 'Schrödinger's quantum cat', *Nature*, **351** (1991), pp. 357ff, cited in George Ellis, 'Ordinary and extraordinary divine action: the nexus of interaction', in Russell *et al.* (eds), *Chaos*, pp. 359–95, p. 370, n. 28.

10 See, e.g., books by the Australian theoretical physicist Gerard Milburn (who tutored me once), in particular *Quantum Technology* (Sydney: Allen & Unwin, 1996) and *The Feynman Processor: An Introduction to Quantum Computing* (Sydney: Allen & Unwin, 1998).

11 David J. Bartholomew, *God of Chance* (London: SCM, 1984), pp. 90–100.

12 *Ibid.*, p. 131.

13 John Polkinghorne, 'The metaphysics of divine action', in Russell *et al.* (eds), *Chaos*, pp. 147–56, p. 152.

14 Thomas Tracy, 'Particular providence and the God of the gaps', in Russell *et al.* (eds), *Chaos*, pp. 289–324, p. 318.

15 Ellis, 'Ordinary and extraordinary', p. 369.

16 Wesley J. Wildman and Robert John Russell, 'Chaos: a mathematical introduction with philosophical reflections', in Russell *et al.* (eds), *Chaos*, pp. 49–90, p. 86.

17 Arthur Peacocke, *Theology for a Scientific Age* (enlarged edn) (London: SCM, 1993), p. 164.

18 *Ibid.*, p. 157.

19 John Polkinghorne, *Science and Providence: God's Interaction with the World* (London: SPCK, 1989), p. 28.

20 Here I extrapolate on comments Polkinghorne makes in *Science*, pp. 28–9, and in 'The metaphysics of divine action', p. 151.

21 Peacocke, *Theology*, p. 54.

22 John Polkinghorne, *Belief in God in an Age of Science* (London: Yale University Press, 1998), p. 61. Note that Arthur Peacocke disputes this possibility of information flow without energy transfer; see Peacocke, *Theology*, p. 370, n. 72.

23 C. G. Jung, *Synchronicity: An Acausal Connecting Principle* (1952) (London: Routledge & Kegan Paul, 1972), p. 44.

24 Keith Ward, *Divine Action* (London: Collins, 1990), pp. 188–9.

25 H. H. Price, *Essays in the Philosophy of Religion* and John Lucas *Freedom and Grace* are cited in a discussion of this option in Brian Hebblethwaite, 'Providence and divine action', *Religious Studies* 14 (1978), pp. 223–6, p. 233; see also John Hick, 'Prayer, providence and miracle', in Michael Goulder and John Hick, *Why Believe in God?* (London: SCM, 1983), pp. 64–80, p. 71. Jung's 'synchronicity' idea was also taken up by the physicist Wolfgang Pauli, and by Arthur Koestler in *The Roots of Coincidence* (London: Hutchinson, 1972); see Michael J. Langford, *Providence* (London: SCM, 1981), p. 82.

26 Peacocke, *Theology*, p. 344.

27 Christopher Mooney SJ, 'Theology and the Heisenberg Uncertainty Principle', in *Theology and Scientific Knowledge: Changing Models of God's Presence in the World* (London and Notre Dame, IN: University of Notre Dame Press, 1996), pp. 71–119, p. 108.

28 John J. Cobb, Jr and David Ray Griffin, *Process Theology: An Introductory Exposition* (1976) (Belfast: Christian Journals Limited, 1977), p. 51.

29 A helpful and widely adopted phrase for which we can thank Austin Farrer, *Faith*, p. 66.

30 Norman Pittenger, *Picturing God* (London: SCM, 1982), p. 82.

31 Polkinghorne, 'The laws of nature and the laws of physics', p. 438.

32 Ruth Page, *God and the Web of Creation* (London: SCM, 1996), p. 55.

33 *Ibid.*, p. 104.

34 *Ibid.*, p. 154.

35 *Ibid.*, p. 170.

36 Polkinghorne, *Science*, p. 34.

37 Farrer, *Faith*, p. 66; cf William C. Placher, *The Domestication of Transcendence: How Modern Thinking About God Went Wrong* (Louisville, KY: Westminster John Knox, 1996), p. 195: 'our lack of understanding of causal mechanisms does not prevent us from attributing agency.'

38 Clayton, *God*, p. 219.

6 Divine Action: Theological Options

*In the relational model God is wise, proficient, resourceful, loving and responsive, even
though God does not get everything he desires.*

John Sanders, *The God Who Risks*, 1998

*We find ourselves called to say things even as we have to admit that we cannot explain
how they all fit together.*

William C. Placher, *The Domestication of Transcendence*, 1996

*Poor, limping world, why does not your kind Creator pull the thorn out of your paw? But
what sort of thorn is this? And if it were pulled out, how much of the paw would
remain?*

Austin Farrer, *Love Almighty and Ills Unlimited*, 1962

*All we go down to the dust;
and, weeping at the grave, we make our song:
alleluya, alleluya, alleluya.*

Contakion of the Departed, Russian Church

'It would seem', writes Owen Thomas, 'that a successful interpretation of
divine activity in the world would involve both a fundamental analogy or
model and a fully elaborated metaphysical theory.'[1] In Chapter 3 we went
part of the way to meeting Thomas' compelling but demanding challenge.
We considered various images of God, including that of God embodied in
the world, and we considered various panentheistic approaches in theology
to accompany them. Thus we began to think analogies and theories. Having
considered aspects of the divine action question in Chapters 4 and 5, we now
push a little further toward the goal Thomas sets, though the 'fully elaborated metaphysics' of which he writes will, I am sure, elude us.

Our task in the lengthy first part of this chapter will be to outline some of
the things that ought to be said about divine action today, in the light of our
discussion so far. Then, and as a 'reality check', the so-called problem of evil
will receive attention. How are we to maintain the tradition's paradoxical
assertion of divine providence in the face of great evil, we postmoderns who
know so well the 'heart of darkness'? This religious recognition of despair
and distortion, of thwarted purpose and bitter disappointment, is never far

from the front of the Judaeo-Christian mind. And here Christian tradition has maintained another paradox, alongside the double agency paradox (of God and God's creatures both being at work in the same actions). This further paradox holds together the bitter facts of natural and human evil with the goodness of God and of God's creation – of God's purposes being trustworthy despite much seemingly needless waste, suffering and heartbreak.

These two paradoxes are part of the grammar of Christian theology, and it is not my intention to offer any resolution of them in what follows. It will be sufficient to bring them into conversation with the world as we now experience it. There is a smugness in some writing at the interface between science and theology today, particularly that touching on the problem of evil, which fails to recognize the impenetrability of these issues. One can point to glib theory in the matter of divine action which is crassly insensitive to suffering among the victims of nature and history, to whom the tradition never presumes to offer merely theoretical relief. But nor does the tradition cease tracing the cords that bind us in these paradoxes, and neither will we in what follows.

Divine action and the context of belief

This discussion began by delineating some important features of contemporary Western experience in Chapter 1, above. The first of these corresponded with what has been called the problem of evil, and I will discuss that later in the chapter. For now, I revisit the other two for, as Philip Clayton rightly insists, 'We must show how assertions of divine activity in the world help to make sense of the human experience of that world.'[2] First there is the relatedness, the holism, the seamless interconnectedness of reality, and our embeddedness in the life of the world. Then, linked to that, there is the secularity of our experience, the down-to-earth 'terrestriality' of our humanity – that we are creatures of the Earth, not exiles from heaven, and that our experience of the sacred comes 'in, with and under' our experience of a life which is in and of the Earth. And this is the case as much symbolically and metaphorically as biologically and socially. *This world* is the one in which God's action is to be conceived.

Divine action and a holistic world-view

Taking the first of these, what sort of divine action sits best with such holistically conceived conditions? We have discounted the 'God does everything', 'God lures everything' and 'God loves everything' options. Uniform divine activity with no special action in response to need and prayer represents an unresponsive God foreign to tradition and experience. Moreover, it accepts that closedness of natural processes and strictness of scientific laws make divine action unlikely, which is an assumption widely questioned in theology's dialogue with science today.

The closed universe and the rigid laws of late seventeenth- and eighteenth-century science made God an absentee creator, or else an interventionist dabbler in a completed creation. With evolutionary science, however, came the possibility of a more extended view of God's creative activity, and the prospect that God led the creative process from within toward ascending complexity, with God or the Spirit of God as its teleological principle. This was uniform divine action, but with special action possible at key turning points, as we noted in the theology of Gordon Kaufman. Such special divine actions could be seen to mark the emergence of new levels of complexity – from inert matter to life, from single to multicellular life, from life to conscious life and from conscious to fully human life. This is still a 'God of the gaps', however. God is invoked to explain how evolutionary advance took place, in the same way that Newton invoked God to explain the yet-to-be-understood, self-correcting nature of planetary orbits. But as Laplace found a satisfactory answer to that one mathematically rather than theologically, so the radical Darwinism of Richard Dawkins claims to account for the evolution of complexity in purely natural terms. So such gaps have once again closed on God. Clearly, this is not a profitable strategy. Ontological gaps are one thing, the possibility of which was considered in the last chapter, but not this invocation of God as a makeshift theory in the onward march of scientific explanation – not this God of epistemological gaps.

Yet despite the need to desist from seeking God in the gaps of cosmic and biological evolution, nevertheless this process of aeons is plainly the way our world came to be where it is and what it is. So this process of aeons must be the way God creates the world, if such is still to be our claim for God. What is more, this is not a world that can be seen to have emerged according to a predetermined plan, unless the plan were very general and non-specific. As far as we can tell, nature has exploited niches, overcoming numerous obstacles and disasters, to give us the present forms of life on Earth. Did God intend the reptilian cataclysm that wiped the Earth of dinosaurs and cleared the way for mammalian life? Or did it just happen, that asteroid impact or whatever it was, so that life expanded to fill the gap in ways not possible before? And if so, is this more likely to be the nature of God's will and the way of God's working – in the overmastering tendency of life to adapt and overcome, rather than in the specific details by which life has taken up its present forms?

According to such a view, God could be seen to create 'in, with and under' the eventual emergence of fertile initial conditions for the cosmos, and for life on Earth to take its eventual course, with the emergence of God-conscious human life as a delightful outcome of processes which allow complexity to emerge but which cannot specify in advance just what forms that complexity will take. So the whole process is seen to be the will of God, and the working of God. God is not the efficient cause of everything, so that the fine design of the human eye, for instance, has to have been present from the beginning in the mind of God, and proof of God's design, as it was for Paley.

Nor does one need to invoke the anthropic principle here, as proof that something extra is needed at the start, in addition to the natural process, to account for the eventual emergence of all the complexity we see – as if God creates like a jigsaw puzzle maker, beginning with the completed picture and then cutting it up into pieces for eventual reassembly. That is, one does not have to identify a major 'gap' at the beginning and declare God to be God of that most crucial gap, from which all the pieces of the jigsaw tumbled, ready for assembly. Countless universes may have come and gone, for all we know, most of them failures that promptly collapsed back into the vacuum field from which they came, or otherwise proved fruitless, until ours came along, as I conjectured in Chapter 1, above. No, God is not to be found in any such epistemological gaps, because science is too good at closing them, with Stephen Hawking every bit as skilled at this in mathematical physics as is Richard Dawkins in evolutionary biology.

But if God is not to be found in the parts, where is God to be found? I suggest that God is discerned in the meaning of the whole, as an interpretation of the whole of the universe, in the light of our human experience, rather than as a theory to explain this bit or that bit of what we see. The world makes itself, in wonderful ways that the likes of Hawking and Dawkins can teach us, without our needing to fear that God is being excluded. Because belief in God is our reaction to the whole, and to our life as part of that whole, rather than a way of explaining this part or that part within the whole. There can always be a natural explanation, for how the eye emerged by evolution from photosensitive cells in folds of skin, for instance, which gave evolutionary advantages to those individuals who fortuitously found themselves possessing them, and so passed them on. There can always be a natural explanation offered even for our own psychological certainties, for experiences that lead us to thoughts of God. Imagining that we live in a closed universe with rigid scientific laws has taught us to seek God in the discontinuities, in the grey areas, in realms of the mysterious. But the tradition of double agency affirmed that God and nature were both at work, seeing no competition in terms of explanation. The newly open universe of twentieth-century science allows this to again be the case.

But there are implications if we discern God in the evolving universe. God becomes creator of a severe and unsympathetic process, by which the fittest survive and the weak are purged. Jürgen Moltmann criticizes this God of evolution as far removed from the God of Jesus Christ. The God of Teilhard de Chardin and Karl Rahner, with Christ as the leading edge of evolution, is not the God of the poor and the downtrodden, according to Moltmann. He writes, 'A *Christus evolutor* without *Christus redemptor* is nothing other than a cruel, unfeeling *Christus selector*, a historical world-judge without compassion for the weak, and a breeder of life uninterested in the victims.'[3] But our world is a process as much of redemption as of creation, forever capitalizing on opportunities, forever taking new directions after mishaps and restarting after calamities. An evolutionary God is a God always creating by constantly redeeming, in the physical, biological and human realms – fertile fields issue from the lava of volcanic eruption, the extinction of dinosaurs favours mammals and humans are regularly raised up on the backs of their disappointments. Of course this is not a state of affairs friendly to the flourishing of every individual creature. The problem of evil, which we discuss in the next section, is built on the recognition of how wasteful this whole planetary experiment is, of how so many undeniable goods emerging in the world process are purchased at the cost of so much suffering. The death of the dinosaurs is part of the price of our being here. And the deaths of however many First World War Turkish infantrymen shot or hacked to death by my grandfather during the famous charge by the Fourth Australian Light Horse on Beer Sheba is part of the price of my own being here to write these words. The world we know is built at a price, and can emerge as far as we know in no other way. To see this as the way of God's creation, even while admitting that there is a strong redemptive dimension to the processes of life, is to part with any sentimentality in our theism, and any naive hope that everything will go nicely for us in life. It is not that sort of world, and we are not that sort of creature.

Divine action and the experience of secularity

The other dimension of experience I mention here is that of secularity, whereby we know ourselves to be creatures of Earth, of history, of economic and political, social and cultural provenance, whose life with God is at the same time the life of Earth. This is the denial of every dualism and every mystification of the true meaning of human life, which is the fulfilment of our embodied personhood rather than its overcoming. There is an element of hiddenness to God which is part of this experience. God is a conclusion from the evidence rather than a piece of the evidence; God is a way of viewing the world rather than something we encounter among other things in the world. The action of God is not a part of our experience, in the same way that other agents are experienced within the causal nexus. We would not expect to assert that God is at work apart from faith, for instance; we would not expect to find objective evidence of God that requires no interpretation and is open to no dispute. This is not to say that God is remote, however. Indeed, one can conceive of God at work everywhere and in everything, according to such a view, without confining God's activity to this outcome, or that. And where a particular encounter with the universal God is asserted, as in Christian claims for the uniqueness of Christ, it is a part that helps us grasp the meaning of the whole, rather than a piece of stand-alone evidence.

The experience of secularity allows the whole of life to be viewed without God, the way of things being fully accounted for by whatever scientific, psychological or socio-economic theory. But it also allows the whole of life to be viewed as encounter with God – a God not of the religious or the spiritual part of life, but rather the whole earthy extent of life. This is the sort of mystical vision which Dietrich Bonhoeffer and other saints of our secular age arrived at – that the modern desacralization of our perception can give rise at a deeper level to a more radical resacralization of the world, which is no longer a world part-natural and part-supernatural, no longer a world of natural continuities and supernatural gaps, and certainly not a closed world into which a remote God intervenes on occasion. The vision of a secular faith is in fact the vision of double agency, in which the world is able to be viewed from two perspectives, one sacred and the other profane. And again, God is a perspective on life in the one world, a way of talking about the meaning and purpose of the whole world process, rather than a contributor to causal processes within that world. Secularity means that there is no action of God in the world. But it does not mean that we cannot see the whole of the world as the action of God. In this connection we recall earlier arguments for the experience of something like double agency in Christian life. While not denying secularity, and the worldliness of experience, nevertheless Christians point to occasions in which their physical and mental actions are experienced as at the same time the action of God. This is not to claim divine intervention into a purely secular life, but to recognize that God is ever at work 'in, with and under' the living of a secular life.

Uniform and special divine action

While I am suggesting that our experience of life today, its holistic interconnectedness and its secularity, is compatible with a double agency view of God's activity, nevertheless there are things I am not suggesting. I am not wanting merely to see the world as God's uniform act and then go no further, content to interpret special divine acts as moments of enhanced perception of God's uniform activity, nor to follow Bultmann and regard divine action as nothing more than the religious self's perspective on a desacralized world. We have taken some trouble in the last chapters to look at options for conceiving divine action, and ended our conversation with recent science by concluding that the world as we understand it is compatible with God being at work in it. But we have wanted to avoid ascribing all the action and all the choices to God at the expense of giving nature its equal due – the 'God does everything' option – just as we have sought to avoid the idea of God as one cause among others – the 'God lures everything' option. We are left with God as the primary cause of everything, but not necessarily so that God's action is wholly background and uniform, without special action having any part to play.

A case for special divine action

The challenge is how to think special and uniform divine action together, in a way that avoids limiting God to epistemological gaps in our understanding of cosmic, terrestrial and human evolution. Thomas Tracy seeks this sort of synthesis, combining the uniformity and hiddenness of God's activity with the tradition's constant affirmation of God at work in the lives of Christians individually and collectively. Here he is worth quoting at length.

> God's dealings with us can go unrecognised, therefore, precisely because they are so integrally and extensively woven into the fabric of our lives. But for this same reason, when we set out to identify God's workings in or upon us, it will be possible to cite a tremendous variety of events as bearing God's influence. The language of Christian practice reflects this. The tradition has characteristically claimed, for example, that God is actively present in the liturgical life of the community (e.g. in hearing God's word in preaching, and in the reception of the sacraments), and in special episodes of religious experience or in deep structures of religious consciousness. In addition, Christians have recognised God's influence in a wide range of episodes from ordinary life that shape what sort of person one becomes, e.g. in insights into the needs or character or experience of others, in the courage to take risks for the sake of justice or love, in moments of joy and wonder or of exhaustion and despair, in nagging dissatisfactions with the character of our attachments, in a drive to deepened self-knowledge and richer relationship with others, in an expansive desire for fullness of life, and so on.[4]

I now want to make a case for special divine action in the world at large, advancing from these premises upon which many Christians would agree – that God changes people.

Scepticism about God performing special acts, or doing miracles, is widespread in the Western world. But many Christians are happy with the notion that God works on their minds and hearts, sending thoughts, changing attitudes, giving guidance. Many would no longer pray for rain, for a particular election result or even in the expectation that a sick person will recover. But Christians do pray that they and others will be strengthened, converted, guided – clearly, widespread scepticism about special divine action in the world at large is not matched by a similar scepticism in the private realm. God's 'miraculous' action can still be retained, provided it is limited to the realm of the 'psychological miracle'.

First, an objection. John Hick tries to account for this sense of God changing us in terms of uniform rather than specific divine action – God guiding us 'not by a psychological miracle but through our own intense desire for light and our readiness to follow it'[5] toward general rather than particular ends. But I fear this is too bland a view to account for experience. We are less eager to pursue the right than Hick confidently supposes. And there is more to how we move along in life than internal teleology – events, 'accidents' and relationships shape us, too, things beyond our control. These are not just events in our minds, but happenings in the 'real', objective world. So if God is to change us, then reflection on how we do in fact change leads us to look as much to external as to internal factors. Hick cannot account for the reality of Christian experience by recourse to uniform divine action alone.

So let us consider the possibility that God influences minds by special action. But immediately there is a further problem. It is assumed to be less problematic for God to operate on or in the mind, but what of the connection between the mind and the brain with which we are increasingly well acquainted? Michael Goulder's sceptical comments about this are helpful here, when he comments on the way God might have been involved in bringing an outcome in the Falklands War. Many would be unhappy with the idea of God deflecting a missile, for instance, but they would be willing to thank God for sustaining the resolve of the Prime Minister and the government in prosecuting the war. But, as Goulder asks, 'what is the difference between God interfering with the electronics of the Exocet, and his interfering with Mrs Thatcher's brain circuits?' He goes on to conclude that 'psychological miracles are just as much miracles as mechanical miracles – indeed, with electronics, the scale is not much different.'[6]

It is a confronting but nevertheless undeniable fact of life that the realm of the personal is also the realm of the chemical and the electrical. Obviously, the mind is not reducible to the chemical or the electrical, but it is influenced by the chemical and the electrical. Hence the efficacy of psychiatric pharmacology and electroconvulsive therapy. How might God influence the mind, change the mind, guide, convict or transform the person, in the light of our recognition that chemical reactions and electric fields are going to be involved?

The possibility of God working mental outcomes through manipulation at the level of quantum events in the brain is today's major contender for an explanation here. It assumes that ideas emanate from brain states, emerging in turn from quantum excitations in the appropriate neurones. This possibility is advanced as a tentative speculation by the leading mathematical physicist Roger Penrose. 'Since there *are* neurones in the human body that can be triggered by single quantum events,' he opines, 'it is not unreasonable to ask whether cells of this kind might be found somewhere in the main part of the human brain.'[7] Elsewhere we find Penrose wondering that if 'it is not too fanciful to suggest that quantum correlations could be playing an operative role over large regions of the brain', then 'Might there be any relation between a "state of awareness" and a highly coherent quantum state in the brain?'[8] This bare possibility becomes a full-blown theory in the hands of Danah Zohar, who advances a quantum mechanical model of consciousness. She postulates a phase shift whereby molecules in the walls of neurones in the brain enter a state of resonance she claims would constitute a Bose-Einstein condensate, which she then surmises might be the ground state of consciousness. This is along the lines of the large-scale quantum synchronicity found in lasers, superfluids and superconductors but, significantly, also in various forms of biological tissue at body temperature. Zohar points also to EEG results, wherein each of the four wave types are coherent despite the many firing neurones giving rise to them, 'suggesting that a long-range coherence binds the firing patterns of individual neurones'.[9]

Thus we might imagine that God is working through quantum events in the cell walls of neurones in the brain. The impact of God bringing about this outcome rather than that outcome at the minute quantum level could blow up into a brain state which would undergird a new insight or a change of mind that might further God's cause in some important way. All this is highly speculative, however, and Zohar gives little explication of these bare bones – of how raw consciousness is built up into the full panoply of our mental life. And of course she has no theological brief. But this possibility is there in theological conversation today – that God can influence minds in a 'bottom-up' way, starting with quantum excitations.

But if we accept an argument from experience, that God acts in a special way by changing people, and then advance from there to conclude that God might achieve that outcome through influencing quantum outcomes in brain cells, then questions about God's special activity on a wider front are well and truly begged. While we might assume that minds and brains are particularly sensitive to such minute influence, and that the potential results of influencing human beings makes this a particularly fruitful focus for divine action, nevertheless it seems arbitrary and unnecessary to limit what God might do at the quantum level to the realm of human brains.

For one thing, brain states radiate electrical energy which will influence reality outside the skull. We know that minute excitations can be amplified within chaotic regimes to yield a harvest of macroscopic effects elsewhere – the so-called 'butterfly effect'. So God giving me a thought would at the same time be God doing things with electrical fields which could have their own knock-on effect independently of me, and perhaps to a significant extent, regardless of what I did with that thought.

More generally, if God is able to influence minds, bringing brain states and hence ideas that would not otherwise take shape, then God is also able to change things in the wider world from how they might otherwise have gone, employing exactly the same sort of activity. Why? Because brains are the same sort of thing as everything else – matter that ultimately rests on a quantum mechanical foundation. There is no special mentalist activity of

God that can be sensibly asserted while denying other special divine acts. A God who can do things in my head can do things anywhere!

And if God can do such special acts more generally, would God refuse to take the opportunity; would God restrict possibilities for influence, especially in a highly complex world where successful outcomes need all the help they can get? Do we not know how much input and coordination is necessary for us to achieve a desired outcome through our own activity – ask a shipping clerk, a chess champion, an impresario. So why would God, if desiring to bring off a certain outcome, be at work only through quantum events in brains – why not also in atmospheric phenomena, in the crystal growth that fatigues metal and the faulty electrical circuit that unaccountably works, all of these actions together shaping a decision, bringing rescuers to a lost sailor, saving a doomed flight, allowing a homicide detective to spot the crucial clue or whatever desirable outcome?

Intercessory prayer

If we allow special action of God, we must ask if such special action might follow requests made to God in intercessory prayer. Christians have long believed that prayer is answered, if not all the time then some of the time. But today, faced by claims of a closed universe and the discouraging problem of evil, many Christians are loath to believe that God answers prayer – even self-styled 'traditional' Christians.

One possibility is that intercessory prayer is efficacious, but relies on uniform divine action only, working through normal natural processes which are not yet fully understood. In the last chapter we encountered a view that the effect of prayer might be through telepathy. A 'fuller physics' may one day account for links from mind to mind and between mind and matter – links that Jung and many others admit.

Another possibility is that pointed out in much contemporary writing and teaching about intercessory prayer, that its point is the wholesome meditative and moral effect it can have on the one who prays. We are told that our offer of prayer contributes to prayer's answer, because we become the sort of people who act in harmony with our prayer. So if we pray for relief in whichever newsworthy trouble spot, for instance, we may find ourselves financially supporting aid efforts there; or if we pray for reconciliation in a relationship, we may find ourselves acting toward the estranged person in reconciling ways. These examples point to very natural, not at all supernatural aspects of prayer. They can be seen as God's work in the indirect, 'uniform' sense whereby all natural and human events are God's work through secondary causes, on double agency principles. So, perhaps we can go some way toward accounting for the efficacy of intercessory prayer without invoking anything apart from uniform divine action.

But if we admit special as well as uniform divine action, then the efficacy of intercessory prayer on God and the world at large becomes a real possibility, and not just as a piece of paranormal phenomena, or a readily explicable influence on the one doing the praying. While God is likely to know what we will intercede for before we do it, simply by knowing us, the fact we pray may be a necessary precursor for the outcome to be granted. This is, after all, the norm with human relationships, that very often it is important for us to vocalize our wishes. It is a welcome thought that God might actually change plans in response to our prayers. Might not God, when possible, give us what we ask for, simply because we ask for it?[10] After all, this is the tenor of teachings about prayer in the Gospels, that God will grant petitions if they are earnest and offered in the name of Christ.

Of course, this may not always be possible, given that other plans and indeed other prayers may be leading God in other directions at the same time. God will not give the anxious bride a fine day for her wedding without weighing up the prayers of however many farmers for rain, and God will certainly not bring snow on a scorching Australian Christmas Day just because the children might like it (and the adults!) – respect for natural conditions and the contradictory wishes of others would prevent God from doing many of the things that people request in prayer.

We must admit, too, that it would not be good for us if we were granted all the requests we made in prayer. If God favourably answered every school-boy's every prayer, it would lead to a world full of roller blades and video games while empty of metronomes and textbooks, not to mention the impact on women's fashions! And surely it is the imperfectly articulated depths of our prayer that God responds to, rather than our many superficial requests which fail to address those depths. Becoming content with one's circumstances may be the eventual answer to a restless prayer for deliverance from them, for instance, or a character-building appointment full of challenge and opportunities to develop fortitude may be God's preliminary answer to a prayer for career advancement.

So prayer can be understood as in keeping with the uniform action of God but also as a part of how God's special action might be prosecuted in the world. But does this mean the suspension of nature's laws?

Miracle

The miraculous suspension of the 'laws of nature' is not a helpful image. God is not a competitor with the way of things in God's world; God is not engaged in a struggle with brute matter to express God's will. The world God creates is the world God honours, and God works for the world's good and that of the world's creatures through the world's own processes. Keith Ward insists, rightly I am suggesting, that 'God cannot both set up a particular game then step in to alter the rules whenever he feels like it.'[11] In this type of case I find one of the key means for dealing with the problem of evil, but more of this in the next section.

Miracle understood as an expression through nature, rather than nature's overcoming, means that God will do many things, but not all things. If God goes with nature, rather than against it, there are certain things that God will not do. So remission from cancer, changes of weather and other natural phenomena where sensitivity to initial conditions is significant and allows for hidden divine action are all reasonable conjectures in faith, while flying nuns, legs growing back and forcing humans to act are not the sorts of things that God does – nuns have done a lot of good on foot, two legs are not essential for profoundly Godly and humane personhood, and respect for the free will of human agents is not a principle that God could abandon without incalculable consequences, not all of them pleasant.

As for the great miracles of the Bible, we can go a long way in fidelity to Scripture with the hermeneutical principle we are here beginning to enunciate. One thing we know for sure, and it is important to remember this if we are to do justice both to the God who acts and to the true nature of the biblical material, is that a lot of elaborated legend is present in the Hebrew Scriptures. The Exodus, for instance, may well have had an historical core. But God's mythical triumph over chaotic elements at the Red Sea is the heart of the story. And the God who created Israel from the chaos of history is later pictured as creating a whole world from the same chaotic waters in the first creation narrative of Genesis.[12] A number of New Testament miracle narratives recall Old Testament stories, directing them toward a validation of Jesus' identity as the unique one from God. Others employ analogy – walking on water, calming storms, appearing transfigured with the heroes of Hebrew faith and unbinding oppressed sons and daughters of the covenant, are all narrative devices testifying to who Jesus is and what Christians can expect as they join his mission. The accounts need to be read as kerygmatic testimony with an eye to what the redactor was wanting to say, rather than as objective, uninterpreted accounts of dispassionate observation, as if they were police reports routinely taken down and carefully but disinterestedly filed.

This allegorical and kerygmatic emphasis is clear in two parts of Jesus' story regularly used as tests for orthodoxy in discussions of miracle. Here I refer to the virginal conception and physical resurrection of Jesus. I think we can affirm the truth of these narratives, and meaningfully speak of God at work from the beginning and after the end of Jesus' life, without recourse to the blunt instrument of literal historicism, or to the thoroughly non-traditional insistence that God is most truly at work when going most violently against the ways of nature.

Narratives of Jesus' conception in Matthew and Luke[13] use gynaecology to point to theology, and in the light of an alternative account of Jesus' call in Mark and of his pre-existence in John[14] these infancy narratives appear to be creative versions of how it might have been, rather than objective records of a bona fide divine overthrow of the biological order, as many eagerly insist.

I would seek a more comprehensive understanding of incarnation than that, however: Jesus, 'born of a woman, born under the law',[15] is God's work first to last and not just at his origin, God's work 'in, with and under' the working of a human life like ours, subject to the same laws of being as our lives. Otherwise, as Gregory of Nazianzus insisted long ago, against Apollinarius, 'what he has not assumed he has not healed',[16] thus asserting the importance of Jesus' full humanity if he is to be understood as saviour – as the one who at last catalyses the right relationship of his human brothers and sisters with God.

And what of Jesus' resurrection? Again, there are many who insist on the miracle of a revived corpse, trailing clouds of glory, as the essence of resurrection faith. But what does the New Testament say about this mysterious and wonderful thing we call resurrection? The resurrection is presented as an extended event that involved seeing the transformed Jesus,[17] knowing his presence as the word is broken open and the bread is shared in Luke's Emmaus road narrative[18] and being commissioned and empowered by Jesus in John's upper room of the last supper where the spirit of Jesus' mission was poured out on the disciples.[19] Without shifting gear, the experience of later individuals and communities is included in what resurrection means – the risen Jesus 'appearing' to Paul 'as to one untimely born',[20] and to the later Johannine community confident with earlier witnesses of 'what we have seen with our eyes, what we have looked at and touched with our hands, concerning the word of life'.[21]

Edward Schillebeeckx helpfully addresses the theory-laden nature of resurrection faith from its inception, understanding these appearances of Jesus as 'Christological seeing'. While it is common nowadays for the concrete literality of the resurrection accounts to be asserted, it is important to note with Schillebeeckx that experience of resurrection, according to the scriptural witness, is varied, involving more than the bare sight and lack of interpretive gloss that passes for 'reality' to the literalistically and rationalistically minded. The experience of resurrection according to the Gospels is threefold,[22] and contains an element of subjectivity – there is an initiative from Jesus himself (i.e. it is a revelation, not an observation), there is an element of acknowledgment[23] and an element of witness or commitment to mission. The resurrection is an experience of conversion to the cause of Jesus Christ which is still enlisting people today, and in its earliest days it included a range of 'believing–seeing' experiences. This is the miracle. And to squeeze it into a far narrower assertion of God's overmastering power to deflect nature is far too unsubtle to grasp the nature of God's working.

Double agency and the image of an embodied God

If the theory toward which we are leaning is one of double agency, of God making the world through the evolving processes of law and randomness that modern physics and biology have uncovered, and if special divine action is to be given a place in the possibilities we are considering, then what analogy are we to employ to help us visualize this theory? Clearly it is a panentheistic approach, and a number of images are available.

Michael Langford, in a useful discussion of providence, tries out various images in an attempt to balance the steady state support characteristic of general providence with the transformation of events entailed by special providence. He seeks both forms of providence within the same seamless process, rather than defining special providence as intervention into the process from without. Langford offers the wind as one analogy, pointing in a way sailors will recognize to the steady pressure of wind (the 'fetch') as well as to unpredictable flurries as illustrating general and special providence. Better still the tide, which is constant despite the unpredictability of the waves. Langford also identifies tidal bores as singularities that emerge from steady state conditions. Another image suggestive of double agency is that of a novelist and a character. While the character is the creation of the novelist, and has no existence apart from the novelist, nevertheless writers know that characters develop a life of their own. The writer can in a sense allow the character to write itself, and to react 'in character' to obstacles or opportunities placed in the way. Austin Farrer insists that as the writer lives the character from within, so God 'is like a good novelist who has the wit to get a satisfying story out of the natural behaviour of the characters he conceives'.[24]

But best of all is the image of the person in their body. Certainly, the fact of willed movements which are at the same time purely natural is a most helpful image for how God could perform special actions in the world, which are at the same time wholly natural actions?[25] And, of course, there are purely autonomic, unconsciously wrought functions of the body, too, which provide a helpful analogy for uniform divine action. Langford mentions breathing among the latter and signing our name among the former.[26]

Some things just keep happening no matter what – without breathing we would die, and without the fundamental structure of things in the world continuing at the level of physics, then nothing would happen at higher levels and the world would cease to be. If God tried to change these things, there would be nothing of our world left. So we might imagine that there are some things that God will not change, because they are essential, in the same way that we cannot stop our breathing, or our endocrine system in its quiet but crucial background work maintaining the state of our bodies. Some bodily activities allow a measure of voluntary control, but cannot be interfered with too much before harm is done. So too with the world, where no doubt there are some areas of possible divine action where continuity of the whole process demands restraint. And lastly there are areas where God might have a lot of freedom to act within the natural parameters of the system, as we do in our bodies. But as we come to know our physical limitations in the area of voluntary action, so God would need to be aware of what the world can and cannot take, and how each action will bring consequences, perhaps throughout the whole universe due to the 'butterfly effect'. Only thus could God achieve certain desirable ends and minimize harm. If I wish to remain adequately functional, I know that too much fatty food and alcohol, and too many hours at the desk, too little sleep and exercise are inimical to that goal. In the same way God could do many more things in the world, but God must work with the limitations of the world and its various creatures in order to assuredly bring whatever desired outcome. Austin Farrer concludes with the right level of diffidence that the *anima mundi* image of God is the most helpful – though it is an image, and that is all. He writes,

> We may say, then, that God's mind lives in all the world as my feeling 'soul' lives in my whole body or, to put it in antique terms, that God acts as the Soul of the World. It is better, by the way, to say '*acts* as the Soul of the World' than to say '*is* the Soul of the World'. For if we say 'is', we seem to be confining God's action to the world he indwells or animates.[27]

And Farrer believes that would make God dependent on the world, compromising the transcendence of God.

So, here at last is our theory and the analogy to support it. The doctrine is panentheistic, of double agency form. The evolutionary God is the general providence at work through a process of complexification and adaptation, but this same God is the special providence bringing certain particular outcomes through natural processes where the way of things allows it. The special actions are most often perceived in the realm of the personal, but we have seen no reason why such actions should not be more general, because the inner and the outer worlds are not separable. There is no reason why we would not expect God to be at work wherever possible to bring outcomes consistent with God's plans, which Christians discern most fully expressed in Jesus Christ. But we recognize that such special acts are constrained by the nature of the world which God is creating. God 'flexes the muscles' from time to time, but must be careful not to stretch them, nor break the world's bones. And, certainly, God must count the cost if an injury to the world or its creatures is to be risked.

It is to the discussion of the significant problem of injury that we now turn. Why does God allow, even cause, so much injury in the world, to the extent that many are driven to atheism by the irreconcilability of flawed and often terrible conditions with faith in a wise and caring creator?

The problem of evil

This is, at least, how it tends to be seen today: bad things in the world tell against a wise and all-powerful creator; events ought to run more smoothly;

suffering is irreconcilable with being cared for cosmically. Ergo, God cannot exist. In answer, believers assert that things are as they are for a reason – that God has to follow the rules of the game, for instance, as Keith Ward has suggested. This case *against* God has been termed naive and immature for expecting God to be an agent of the nice life affluent Westerners now expect. This case *for* God has been termed 'cosmic toryism', a theology of the status quo, seeking to draw a veil of purpose over the horror of life. Neither case can bear the paradox of evil, a central feature of the Judaeo-Christian tradition – that it is God's world, but also a world of evil and suffering.

'The Horror! The Horror!'

The fact of evil was recognized as a problem for belief in God in classical antiquity, and also in the Hebrew Scriptures. But in the Bible there is no atheism, as there is in antiquity. We do find a sense of God's covenant faithfulness, however, and various attempts to explain why things go badly for Israel. The Deuteronomic history, from Joshua to 2 Kings, is one such attempt, suggesting that infidelity in Israel is the cause of God allowing misfortune to come upon it. But the revisionist theology of the book of Job puts an end to that. Here is a just and upright man who is nevertheless a victim of the worst imaginable suffering, and yet he trusts God. So it is in the psalms, which are not embarrassed by lament, by calling God to account, yet do so in the context of praise and hopefulness. For the suffering of individuals, for the huge theological problem of the exile and for the unpunished thriving of the wicked, the psalms call out the paradox that all of this is bitter, galling truth, and yet 'the mercy of the Lord endures forever'. The frank honesty of the psalms is something we rarely find in the Churches today, where a positive thinking mentality often passes for biblical faith and hope. As Walter Brueggemann reminds us, however, 'a church that goes on singing "happy songs" in the face of raw reality is doing something very different from what the Bible itself does.'[28] Yet such an attitude goes with the tenor of modern Christianity, which has sought a rational account for the fact of evil.

Attempts to give a rational account for the presence of evil in a good creation are not a new thing.[29] Augustine started a prominent tradition which viewed evil as the absence of good, operating like the shadows which help bring a picture's colours to clear visibility. Aquinas expects that a world created by the perfect God will be less than perfect. And he knows that there are competing goods – between predators and prey, as between the path to comfort and survival on the one hand, and the path to martyrdom on the other.[30] Both believed in a principle of plenitude that saw God's glory reflected best in a world teeming with as many different sorts of creature as possible, some of which are unavoidably harmful.

But the turning point in Christian attitudes, as we have noted elsewhere in our study, came in the light of the seventeenth century. There the rise of science made the intricacy of creation clearer, and the question of why the world was not more efficient came to be raised. In the eighteenth century theodicy emerged as a new departure in Augustine's project: how to justify events such as the catastrophic Lisbon earthquake and tsunami, which killed over 60,000 on All Souls' Day in 1755, in the light of God's good creation? There was, for instance, Liebniz's *Theodicy* (1710), with what Hick calls his 'cybernetic myth' – that God had taken infinite pains to set up what is in effect 'the best of all possible worlds'. For Liebniz, according to Hick, the problem of evil 'was an intellectual puzzle rather than a terrifying threat to all the meaning that he had found in life'.[31] Here we are plainly a long way from the psalmists and from Job, though we are not too far from Job's comforters.

William Placher declares such Enlightenment attempts at justifying God in the face of suffering and evil to be morally tone-deaf, preferring as they do a neat natural theology to something that might actually engage with the shock of disaster, tragedy, evil and futility as it is felt, and be of some pastoral use to the afflicted. The Bible does not explain suffering, but it does offer a myriad of instances whereby God reassures people in their suffering, or else overcomes the causes of it.[32] This is the twin focus of the pastoral ministry, after all, which while open to the use of analysis to aid a liberating self-understanding, does not tend to offer theoretical relief for real-life problems. 'The cornerstone of theodicy', however, 'is the attempt to provide a *teleology* of evil and suffering,' writes Kenneth Surin, 'to slot occurrences of evil and suffering into a scheme of things consonant with the essentially rational workings of divine providence.'[33] And of course this has a political dimension, the 'cosmic toryism' I mentioned earlier. Theodicy like this is complicit in a culture of instrumental control by the strong, who are in charge of meaning, with little to offer those on the underside of history but Marx's opium of the people. It is the triumph of political and cultural orthodoxy committed to rational control over the ill-fitting facts of life. 'Theodicy in the theoretical mode', insists Stanley Hauerwas, 'is but the metaphysical expression of the deep-seated presumption that our belief in God is irrational if it does not put us on the winning side of history.'[34]

This is plainly the modern project at work, steaming up the wild river of history like the inadequate little boat that bore Marlow toward Conrad's 'Heart of Darkness', into the complexity, the moral ambiguity, the surdlike obstinacy of so much we now recognize in the wilderness of life. Postmodern culture is rushing to frolic in this vacuum, of course, like Conrad's Mistah Kurtz. As Christians we choose not to join this cousin of Nietzsche's 'overman' in his revels, but we share with Marlow his impression that Kurtz *is* remarkable, remarkable for being able to look where Marlow and the world he represents, a civilized, ordering world, has been loath to look – 'into the heart of an immense darkness'.[35]

It is into something like this darkness that Job went, and there he was offered something like theodicy by his three comforters. Postliberal commentators unite in condemnation of their strategy, while they honour Job[36] for maintaining his faith, despite its fragmentariness, despite its lack of closure, before the heart of darkness. As with many of us, Job is forced to enlarge the meaning-supplying narrative that had adequately served him hitherto, as a result of experience. As Kenneth Surin puts it, in his perceptive reflection on Job,

> Job begins to 'write' this more comprehensive narrative when he starts to formulate his rejoinders to his comforters. It is a narrative which shows Job to have moved beyond the faith of his fathers to a new kind of faith, a faith in which Job turns in real hope to the God who speaks 'out of the whirlwind', that is, the holy mystery who is heard through the categories of the concealed, the unexplained, the arbitrary. His experience has compelled him to tread the path of unknowing. God refuses to give Job the explanations he craves, and Job has to work towards a faith beyond all personal concerns. In repenting of his stupidity in speaking of things that he cannot understand (40: 3–5; 42: 1–6), Job learns that he has to love and worship this hidden and unknowable God for God's own sake.[37]

Surin insists that the Christian answer to evil and suffering is what he calls a 'second-order theological discourse', a stammered response to the world's cry of pain deeply heard, rather than any slick, overconfident rejoinder. And that cry of pain is the 'first-order discourse' to which he would have us attend. It is the cry of godforsaken, dehumanized victims of the crassest human cruelty and indifference in the Holocaust, for instance, which mocks our pious dreams of closure. But it is also the struggle for liberation that wells up with that cry. Rather than a theodicy, the best Surin sees us offering is 'a second-order theological discourse ranging over a first-order praxis-generating discourse' which ensures that our theological talk will be chastened by the reality of suffering, and shaped by our proper practical response to it.

Reaping the whirlwind

But does such a chastened stance before the victims, does such embrace of their struggle, mean that theological reflection on their plight is wholly inappropriate? Does not sympathy wonder at causes, and solidarity seek a firmer purchase for its activism through analysis? The postliberal project delights in paradox, and certainly a measure of paradox is ultimately inescapable. But are we barred from all clarity? Can we not demarcate more clearly the area of paradox? Indeed, perhaps by reflection we can sharpen the paradox.

Austin Farrer is one with a profound respect for the mystery of a suffering which defies being mapped let alone solved. Yet he is not in favour of throwing up our hands in a too hasty invocation of paradox. He agrees that Job's comforters have trivialized the fact of evil, but by their insistence that our troubles punish us or do us good they show themselves mendacious, not merely wrong – they rush to justify evil in their justification of God, therein misrepresenting the God whose response to evil is anything but theoretical, along with silencing any pity they might have felt. 'Through faults both of intellect and character, Job's comforters mismanage their task,' Farrer readily admits, 'but it is a proper enough task in itself.'[38] I suggest, then, that attempts to understand divine action illuminated by the problem of evil can continue, and that they need not degenerate into heartless speculation.

If we must, with Job, weave a new narrative for faith in confronting the fact of evil, then we must not forget our need for faith narratives to reflect engagement with recent science as well. God-talk is shaped and chastened by our encounter with evil, to be sure, but so too is it influenced by our encounter with quantum physics, chaos theory, emergent complexity, evolutionary biology and all the other scientific realms we have been examining. Indeed, science explains the cause of much natural evil and can help overcome the ill effects, so that dialogue with science is not totally divorced from dialogue with the facts and experiences of human and animal suffering, not to mention the liberating struggle against them. It seems incongruous, then, that we will listen to the call for liberation from suffering, which must if serious seek to analyse causes of suffering, and even ask of science how particular forms of suffering might be avoided or overcome, but not seek scientific insights in our attempt theologically to understand these facts of suffering and natural evil.

At the end of our discussion in the last chapter, we found ourselves able to admit possibilities for thinking divine action in the world that had escaped our more rationalistic forebears, though without being clear about the exact nature of that action, or of any 'causal joint' between God and the world. But because not much can be said does not mean that nothing can be said. So without denying the important pastoral and theological correctives of the postliberal critique of theodicy, and indeed on the way to their critical restatement, I want to offer some 'third-order theological discourse', reflecting on the chastened 'second-order discourse' which Surin will allow us. I mention two key types of argument common in theological discussions of evil and suffering. One of these affirms God's commitment to the freedom of persons and processes, to be themselves without interference, come what may. The other recognizes that good can come out of suffering.

In dealing with human evil, a standard theodicy is the so-called 'free will defence' of Alvin Plantinga. This is a classic argument, to the effect that a world with humans acting freely in it is a better world than one in which humans are constrained in some way to always pursue the good. According to this Augustinian view, we are stuck with the possibility that humans will wreak evil and suffering on the world because an alternate world where such things will not happen is an inferior world, and hence a less fit object for God's creating.[39] There is no obvious parallel in the animal world to the 'free will defence', such that animal suffering might be offset by some moral gain it allowed. But John Polkinghorne does apply something like the 'free will defence' to God's dealings with the cosmos as a whole. His so-called 'free process defence' is an elegant and helpful way of stating the conviction that has undergirded all our discussions of divine action, that God honours the world and works in accordance with its natural processes. That it is a better world in which things go their own way, rather than a world in which God manipulates everything directly apart from secondary causes, is a point we have seen Aquinas make – such a world is unworthy of a great creator. So it is, too, in Polkinghorne's updated statement of this ancient conviction.[40]

With this style of defence goes an idea much older, that suffering and difficulty can produce character and maturity – an assessment sometimes true, though admittedly often false. Such a world is a 'vale of soulmaking', in which God lets us face unpleasant challenges for our own good, and does not 'give it to us easy'. This is of course a classic instance of 'cosmic toryism', and while we admit its potential correctness for some situations and some people, we recognize a world of damaged and embittered victims who tell a different tale. But again, human evil is not the whole story. Great waste and carnage is the way of animal life, too, and animal pain is no more justifiable by a 'vale of soulmaking' argument than it is by a 'free will defence' in the form it is applied to humans. In one of its furthest and most breathless reaches, theodicy has even sought to justify God by denying the reality of animal pain.[41] Other writers on the subject admit its reality but try to soften the blow somewhat, like Farrer, for whom

> The God of nature gives his animal creatures pains out of love for them, to save their lives; he makes the way of destruction distasteful to them, as a parent makes the path of danger distasteful to a child, by little punishments. Again, out of love for them, God moves his creatures to shun their pains and mend their harms, so far as their sense and capacity allows. And at last, when they must acknowledge defeat, as every perishable creature must, he relieves them of the power and will to struggle, of the pain on stimulus of which they can no longer usefully act, and of the being they can no longer hopefully defend.[42]

These approaches recognize something potentially positive in suffering – it is understood in both human and animal cases as potentially for the greater good, though it may not seem so in every case.

In the light of these key arguments, my question, which will not lead to a full-blown theodicy, but which might stall God's dismissal on grounds of culpability, is this: how much can we expect God to change, to deal with the world's suffering, before it ceases to be the world we know? Let us explore this idea for a moment.

To remove cancer, God would have to remove the capacity for cells to mutate, which would have enormous implications for cell biology – in the area of advantageous mutations, for instance, on the basis of which natural selection takes place and life evolves. Without a great deal of carnage in the realm of individual creatures and without the extinction of species there would be no human beings on the Earth, because we and all higher life forms have emerged through evolution, through this same brutal path of natural selection. If there were any other way for us to have arisen from lower forms of life, short-circuiting this extraordinary but also fearful process, then it is quite inconceivable to us. And what would we be like if we did not come up from animal life through evolution, bearing the marks of that process as part of our being? The pleasures of animal life – eating, sleeping, nesting, mating, playing, competing, fighting, marking and protecting territory – are our pleasures, and while we feel bound to rise above the worst excesses of our animal natures, our 'original sin', nevertheless we would not be who we are without it.

We would not be who we are without it . . . This is a key insight. Austin Farrer puts it with unescapable clarity: 'We could only wish the world to be made otherwise, if we could wish to be creatures of another sort.'[43] This is an insight calling on the holistic understanding we now have of reality. What *could* God change? Could God suspend the laws of nature so things did not interfere and harm was not done? But surely reality is a nexus of relating, and significant interference is the essence of life and fulfilment within that nexus, as well as the means of death and suffering.

I think the point is made. This is *our* world, as much because of its faults as in spite of them. We are part of the world, and a different world would scarcely be likely to support or give rise to human life. The conditions of the world, suffering included, are the conditions of our humanity. And so it is for our fellow creatures as well. This is not a theodicy of the sort the postliberals rightly question. It is a sober theological reflection on the limits of our understanding, in keeping with their critique of slick, control-obsessed, heartless affirmations that all suffering and evil is for a purpose. It is a reflective adherence to the paradox of God creating the world, but that world containing evil – a paradox the tradition has traced, but which at its best it never claimed to resolve.

Notes

1 Owen Thomas, 'Summary analysis', in Thomas (ed.), *God's Activity in the World: The Contemporary Problem* (American Academy of Religion, 'Studies in Religion' Series, no. 31; Chico, CA: Scholars Press, 1983), pp. 231–40, p. 234.

2 Philip Clayton, *God and Contemporary Science* (Edinburgh Studies in Constructive Theology) (Grand Rapids, MI: Eerdmans, 1997), p. 203.

3 Jürgen Moltmann, *The Way of Jesus Christ: Christology in Messianic Dimensions* (1989) (London: SCM, 1990), p. 296. Here he is reacting to views of God at work such as those of Teilhard de Chardin SJ, *The Phenomenon of Man* (London: Collins, 1959) and Karl Rahner SJ, in 'Christology within an evolutionary view of the world', *Theological Investigations 5: Later Writings* (London: Darton, Longman & Todd, 1966), pp. 157–92. A useful recent discussion of the issue is provided by a Roman Catholic colleague of mine, Denis Edwards, in *The God of Evolution: A Trinitarian Theology* (Mahwah, NJ: Paulist, 1999).

4 Thomas F. Tracy, 'Narrative theology and the acts of God', in Brian Hebblethwaite and Edward Henderson (eds), *Divine Action: Studies Inspired by the Philosophical Theology of Austin Farrer* (Edinburgh: T. & T. Clark, 1990), pp. 173–96, p. 191.

5 John Hick, 'Prayer, providence and miracle', in Michael Goulder and John Hick, *Why Believe in God?* (London: SCM, 1983), pp. 64–80, p. 77.

6 Michael Goulder, 'The action of God', in *Why Believe*, pp. 81–96, p. 84.

7 Roger Penrose, *The Emperor's New Mind: Concerning Computers, Minds and the Laws of Physics* (1989) (London: Vintage, 1990), p. 517.

8 Roger Penrose, 'Minds, machines and mathematics', in Colin Blakemore and Susan Greenfield (eds), *Mindwaves* (Oxford: Blackwell, 1987), p. 274, cited in Danah Zohar, *The Quantum Self* (London: HarperCollins, 1990), p. 61.

9 Zohar, *Self*, p. 70.

10 So suggest two normally hard-headed British theologians (perhaps indulgent parents): see John Polkinghorne, *Science and Providence: God's Interaction with the World* (London: SPCK, 1983), p. 72; Keith Ward, *Divine Action* (London: Collins, 1990), p. 162.

11 Ward, *Divine Action*, p. 112.

12 Gerhard von Rad, *Old Testament Theology*, Vol. 1 (1957) (London: SCM, 1975), pp. 178–9; Bernard F. Batto, 'The Reed Sea: *Requiscat in Pace*', *Journal of Biblical Literature*, **102** (1983), pp. 27–35.

13 Matthew 1.18–23; Luke 1.26–38.

14 Mark 1.9–11; John 1.1–18.

15 Galatians 4.4.

16 Gregory of Nazianzus, *Ep.*, ci., excerpted in Henry Bettenson, *Documents of the Christian Church* (2nd edn) (Oxford: Oxford University Press, 1963), p. 45.

17 Mark 16.9–18; Matthew 28.16–20; Luke 24.36–49; John 20.11–29.

18 Luke 24.13–35.

19 John 20.19–23.

20 1 Corinthians 15.8.

21 1 John 1.1.

22 Edward Schillebeeckx OP, *Jesus: An Experiment in Christology* (1974, ET 1979) (London: Collins [Fount] 1983), p. 353.

23 Those who insist on an objective sighting view of the resurrection foreign to the

texts would do well to meditate on Matthew 28.17: 'When they saw him, they worshipped him: but some doubted.'

24 Austin Farrer, *A Science of God* (London: Geoffrey Bles, 1966), p. 76; cf. Placher, *The Domestication of Transcendence* (Louisville, KY: Westminster John Knox, 1996), p. 125.

25 Thomas F. Tracy, 'Particular providence and the God of the gaps', in Robert John Russell, Nancey Murphy and Arthur R. Peacocke (eds), *Chaos and Complexity: Scientific Perspectives on Divine Action* (2nd edn) (Vatican City State: Vatican Observatory Publications; Berkeley, CA: The Center for Theology and the Natural Sciences, 1997), pp. 289–324, p. 307.

26 Michael J. Langford, *Providence* (London: SCM, 1981), p. 70. Other uses of personal agency are widespread in the literature, e.g. Arthur Peacocke on the suitability of this image for his 'top-down' emphasis in *Theology for a Scientific Age* (enlarged edn) (London: SCM, 1993), p. 161; also Clayton, *God*, p. 264.

27 Farrer, *Science*, p. 85.

28 Walter Brueggemann, *The Message of the Psalms: A Theological Commentary* (Minneapolis, MN: Augsburg, 1984), pp. 51 or 52, cited in Stanley Hauerwas *Naming the Silences: God, Medicine and the Problem of Suffering* (Grand Rapids, MI: Eerdmans, 1990), p. 81.

29 The standard work on the problem of evil in its classical and contemporary forms is John Hick, *Evil and the God of Love* (1966) (2nd edn, new Preface; London: Macmillan, 1985). In the paragraph to follow I am indebted to his discussions in Chapters 4, 5 and 7.

30 *Summa theologiae*, 1a.22.2ad2, cited in Placher, *Domestication*, p. 116.

31 Hick, *Evil*, p. 154.

32 Placher, *Domestication*, pp. 204–9.

33 Kenneth Surin, *Theology and the Problem of Evil* (Signposts in Theology Series; Oxford: Blackwell, 1986), p. 53.

34 Hauerwas, *Naming*, p. 56; cf my comments on 'the ideological captivity of theism' in Chapter 2, above.

35 Joseph Conrad, *Heart of Darkness* (1902) (London: Penguin Classics, 1983), p. 121.

36 Placher, *Domestication*, p. 207; Hauerwas, *Naming*, p. 45.

37 Surin, *Theology*, pp. 26–7.

38 Austin Farrer, *Love Almighty and Ills Unlimited* (1962) (London: Collins, 1966), p. 16.

39 Alvin Plantinga, 'The free will defence', in M. Black (ed.), *Philosophy in America* (London: Allen & Unwin, 1965), pp. 204–20.

40 Polkinghorne, *Science*, pp. 66–7.

41 Peter Harrison, 'Theodicy and animal pain', *Philosophy*, **64** (1989), pp. 79–92.

42 Farrer, *Science*, p. 102.

43 *Ibid.*, p. 61.

Afterword

In this study we have sought to move beyond the God of classical theism and 'His' (very much 'His') atheistic shadow. The tradition long knew a God related to the world, expressed through the world and honouring the world. Modern science led to problems when theology forgot this tradition, however, leaving us a God severed from the world and subsequently severed from imagination and belief. But modern science has more recently helped to recover the possibility of thinking of God in relation to the world. Holistic thinking and secular sensibility both reflect the sense we are gaining that this one world is our world, that we are integrally part of a cosmic, fifteen-billion-year dance of randomness and stability, in which we come to discern a meaning, a purpose, a personal reality, which we call God – a God we sense summoning us to join that creative, redemptive work which is the essence of this whole cosmic process. This is a God we appreciate as *panentheistic*, rather than *theistic* or *pantheistic*, and which we imagine in a variety of organic ways, the most suggestive being that of God embodied in the world. Modern science has of late also begun to relax the tight rigidity of its laws – the world may indeed be a place in which God can work, in ways where faith is evoked but sense is not assaulted nor overwhelmed.

With the possibility *that* God works, though with little clarity about the mechanisms of *how* God works, we have speculated on the sort of things God might be doing in the world. The model that the tradition most consistently gives is that of double agency, and we have begun to reimagine it for today. And this on the analogy of our own experience, in two ways – first, that Christians at times know themselves to be acting independently yet sense at the same time that they are wholly the instrument of God and, second, by analogy with our embodied experience, which enables us to think of primary and secondary causality because of the way we move our bodies. As for God's special action, we noted the conviction of Christians everywhere that God guides us in our inner lives, and then on the basis of that holism which is a leitmotif of our discussion, we found no good reason why God's special action should be confined to things happening within human minds and brains.

Then, finally, in discussions of the problem of evil, we considered another key Christian paradox, in addition to that of double agency: the conviction that God is at work creating and redeeming, even though things frequently seem incompatible with any such activity. We recognized that theodicy reflects a modern attempt to bring the complexity and intractability of this fact under rational control, even harnessing God to the status quo. While admitting the paradox is not resolvable, nevertheless we respectfully considered the question of how the world might be made differently, concluding that if God began changing things, our profoundly interrelated world would quickly become a different sort of world, unimaginably so, and us with it.

The God emerging from these reflections acts through the world for its creation and redemption in accord with the world's own nature, preserving free processes and free will. Moreover, this is a God who strives with creation to bring good out of evil. Christians sense this in their own lives, and most fully in the story of Jesus, who comes alive for us in Scriptures, liturgies, sacraments, lives and communities of transformation and hope. Because we can imagine God working in these ways, and because the sense of Jesus alive among Christians confirms our belief, we can imagine God working as Christ did, in bitterness, failure, disaster, bringing new opportunities for life and hope, never abandoning the individual for the sake of the process, but neither abandoning the process and the countless other individuals forming part of it.

The God of Jesus Christ is a God who is no stranger to the heart of darkness – a God able to turn secularity into mysticism and evil into the seedbed of hope. The God who plumbs the depths of hell on Good Friday is the only God who can pass inspection by the victims of history, driven to atheism by evil and suffering. This God, I am suggesting, is poured out in solidarity with a much loved world, and is doing everything possible for that world without making it impossible for that world to continue in accord with its own being. It is in the light of this divine solidarity that the Church proclaims 'the resurrection of the dead, the murdered and the gassed',[1] of which God's redemptive activity in the present is a foretaste. This is a God beyond theism and atheism, whose way of creation is through risk and failure and creative advance, and always through solidarity with a beloved world – *this* world.

Notes

1 Jürgen Moltmann, *The Crucified God: The Cross of Christ as the Foundation and Criticism of Christian Theology* (1973) (London: SCM, 1974), p. 275.

Index